Getting into Graduate School in the Sciences

A Step-by-Step Guide for Students

Are you applying for graduate school and feeling overwhelmed by the choices available to you and the complexity of the application process? This informative and humorous guide for life and earth science students offers comprehensive advice to help you prepare and increase your chances of success. Adopting a step-by-step approach, you will be guided through the entire application process, from undergraduate preparation and choice of graduate program, to funding, applying, scheduling a visit, and finally deciding which offer to accept. Based extensively on a comprehensive survey of graduate admissions programs across the United States, the advice offered is evidence-based and specific to the natural sciences. This jargon-free text ensures that prospective students are well prepared and make best use of all available resources to convince graduate programs and advisors that you are the best candidate.

S. Kersey Sturdivant, Ph.D., is a marine scientist who specializes in human disturbance of the benthic environment. He is a faculty member at Duke University, USA and helped establish an environmental consulting company, INSPIRE Environmental, which focuses on environmental impact assessments of the seafloor. In his spare time he blogs about science at SouthernFriedScience.com, and you can follow him on twitter @Wormcam.

Noelle J. Relles, Ph.D., is a marine scientist who specializes in landscape mapping of coral reef habitats. She received her doctorate at the College of William & Mary's Virginia Institute of Marine Science where she studied Caribbean coral reefs and marine policy.

Getting into Graduate School in the Sciences

A Step-by-Step Guide for Students

S. Kersey Sturdivant
Duke University, USA
INSPIRE Environmental, LLC

Noelle J. Relles
The State University of New York
at Cortland, USA

CAMBRIDGE
UNIVERSITY PRESS

University Printing House, Cambridge CB2 8BS, United Kingdom

Cambridge University Press is part of the University of Cambridge.

It furthers the University's mission by disseminating knowledge in the pursuit of
education, learning and research at the highest international levels of excellence.

www.cambridge.org
Information on this title: www.cambridge.org/9781107420670

First published 2017

Printed in the United States of America by Sheridan Books, Inc.

A catalogue record for this publication is available from the British Library

Library of Congress Cataloguing in Publication data
Names: Sturdivant, S. Kersey, author. | Relles, Noelle J., author.
Title: Getting into graduate school in the sciences : a step-by-step guide
for students / S. Kersey Sturdivant, Noelle J. Relles.
Description: Cambridge, United Kingdom: Cambridge University Press, 2017. |
Includes bibliographical references and index.
Identifiers: LCCN 2016026764 | ISBN 9781107420670 (paperback)
Subjects: LCSH: Universities and colleges – United States – Graduate
work – Admission. | Universities and colleges – United States – Entrance
requirements. | Science – Study and teaching (Graduate) – United States.
Classification: LCC LB2371.4.S79 2016 | DDC 378.1/55–dc23
LC record available at https://lccn.loc.gov/2016026764

ISBN 978-1-107-42067-0 Paperback

This book is dedicated to our most awesome friends from graduate school (CFelts, Lynn, Asheley, Spoon, Fozzi, Aaron, & Double D), who showed us how to love you, love life, 24/7!

Contents

Preface

"Opaque," "deceiving," "exciting," "tedious," "match-making," and "purgatory." These are just a few of the terms that have been used to describe the graduate school application process, and these varied responses provide an indication of just how innately unique the graduate school application process can be for the natural sciences. Graduate school is itself a curious yet often rewarding intellectual journey of an individual's pursuit to further their mastery in a specific discipline. Curious in the literal sense, as students attempt to elucidate unknowns within their field of study, but also figuratively, because often a student's progress toward graduation (or lack of it) can be perplexing. Before you can experience this journey you must first surmount the most obvious hurdle, graduate school acceptance, which can be a deceptively awkward and tricky proposition. This is particularly true in the natural sciences (which encompasses the earth and life sciences) where students are vying not just for the approval of their prospective graduate institutions, but often also that of a major professor; an underlying uniqueness about graduate school in the sciences, that differs from graduate school in business, law, or medicine. In order to achieve acceptance, there are a number of seemingly obvious, but also many cryptic tactics that a student can employ. The purpose of this book is to ensure that you, as the prospective student, are well prepared, and knowledgeable of all the resources at your disposal, so that you can convince graduate programs and advisors that you are indeed the best candidate.

This book achieves this goal by taking a step-by-step comprehensive approach that marries humor with empiricism. We have surveyed hundreds of graduate programs in the natural sciences and used the information we gathered from these programs to derive the conclusions in our book, and provide systematic suggestions of how applicants can best position themselves for acceptance. As a result, this book is more than just instructional anecdotes, but provides a window into the thinking of graduate admissions offices. Our survey was completed by 235 natural science graduate programs in the USA, and received responses from a large portion of the top Institutes of Higher Education (IHE) in the USA. Respondents consisted of 4 of the 8 Ivy League universities, 135 R1 programs (research-focused IHE), 72% of the top 25 IHEs, 74% of the top 50 IHEs, and 73% of the top 100 IHEs. Broken down by discipline, 37% of respondents were from biology (typically life sciences programs), 29% were chemistry, 21% were physical science, and 13% were environmental science. Some of the IHEs requested acknowledgment and can be found in the acknowledgments section.

An important note regarding the survey and presentation of results as you read through this book. Some simple statistics are used to explain and signify the importance of the results obtained from our national survey of graduate programs. To enable a quick understanding of what analyses were conducted and what they mean, we briefly provide a description. After surveying hundreds of graduate programs in the natural sciences, the programs were divided into various groups to assess if there were differences in responses by programs (e.g. life vs. earth sciences, top 100 vs. other, research 1 vs. non-research-focused programs). As a result of these distinctions, occasionally the results presented in this book contrast the average responses between the aforementioned groups to highlight similarities/differences. Differences are considered significant (i.e. the variation or the differences between observation is real and worthy of attention) if the p-value is less than 0.05. To indicate these differences, p-values less than 0.05 are presented as an asterisk (*). Numerous asterisks indicate the severity of significance, e.g. $p < 0.005$ (**), and $p < 0.0005$ (***).

In this book, we briefly discuss course selection and preparation during the undergraduate career, but specifically outline the graduate school application process from the initial application to acceptance into a program. We also include specific discussions geared toward students who are applying to graduate school after taking time off between undergraduate and graduate school, international students, and students from underrepresented groups.

This book is designed as an informative and humorous "how-to guide" for undergraduate students and postgraduates. It provides information and guidance on applying to USA-based graduate schools, for research and thesis-based program in the natural sciences, as opposed to a clinical program or non-thesis study. The natural sciences are branches of science that strive to elucidate the rules governing the natural world through the use of empirical scientific methods; empirical denoting information garnered through observation or experimentation. The list of disciplines that this book covers (illustrated below) is by no means meant to be exclusive, but is representative of the graduate program structures definitively covered by this book. It is very likely that the advice provided in this book covers many aspects of graduate programs not included on this list (e.g. social science programs that focus on human-environment dimensions). The following is an inclusive list of natural science graduate programs:

Anatomy	Animal behavior	Atmospheric science	Biomedical science
Biochemistry	Biodynamics	Bioinformatics	Biology
Cell biology	Chemistry	Developmental biology	Earth science
Ecology	Environmental science	Evolutionary biology	Evolutionary genetics
Genetics	Geology	Immunology	Marine science
Microbiology	Molecular biology	Neuroscience	Oncology
Parasitology	Pathology	Physics	Physiology
Plant sciences	Structural biology	Systems biology	Zoology

Most books written about graduate school do a poor job of detailing the application process for students interested in studying the natural sciences. The books are either not based on thesis/research programs, not focused on natural sciences students, ignore nontraditional students, are outdated, are solely opinion-based, discuss other aspects of graduate school more specifically, do not mention the importance of establishing an advisor/advisee relationship, or, more commonly, a combination of these characteristics. Our book addresses a lack of instructional preparation for graduate education in the natural sciences, and attempts to do so empirically and lightheartedly with input from hundreds of ranked graduate admissions programs around the USA. While many students realize the obvious necessity of maintaining a high Grade Point Average (GPA) and scoring well on the Graduate Record Examination (GRE), these facets make up only a small portion of the qualities and requirements that increase the probability of acceptance into a graduate program. For example, many students may not realize the weight placed on establishing a relationship with potential advisors and the awkwardness of attempting to establish said relationship with a revered scientist one has never met; our book will include helpful tips to navigate and establish rapport despite this uneasiness. Also throughout this book, when referring to a major advisor, a few terms are used that are synonymous. Major advisor can also be described as an advisor or Principal Investigator (PI).

Additionally, this book will take time to focus on women and minorities in science. Science has been traditionally a Caucasian male-dominated discipline, but in recent years the presence of women and minorities has grown. A number of funding opportunities exist solely for these groups, and our book will discuss how to take advantage of these prospects to further the likelihood of acceptance into a graduate program. In addition to specifically addressing women and minorities in the application process, as needed, each chapter will include a section directed at international students applying to graduate school in the USA. There are extra steps that international students will need to take care of with regard to applying, such as having transcripts sent as part of the application package and traveling internationally to visit potential schools. International students will also need to give special consideration to relevant deadlines and the availability of funding for non-US citizens.

Finally, as you go through your graduate school application process try to keep in mind two important things: 1) While it is a daunting endeavor, try and have fun. When applying to graduate school you will have the opportunity to engage with some truly interesting people, as well as some very awkward ones, many of whom will be esteemed (or headed in that direction) in their specific careers. Use the opportunity to hone your skills in developing the best way to "sell" yourself, as this is a trait you will have to call on throughout your career. Also enjoy the visits, as they will sometimes provide the opportunity to visit a place you have never been to before, and to interact with people you may never see again. 2) This book IS NOT the Bible. That is to say, this is not Zombie Land, and these are not rules to live by. Please remember that this book is providing guidance and advice based on the average experience, but in the end, you need to take what you learn from this book and apply it to your own specific circumstances. A lot of the advice provided in this book can and should be taken as it is literally stated, but please use common-sense logic when taking into account some of the advice offered. The only universal truth is that each person's experiences will undoubtedly differ, and as a result everything in this book cannot be directly translated to your experience. With that ... let's begin!

Acknowledgments

There are a large number of people and entities to thank for support in allowing this book to come to fruition. Each are listed on the next page, but we wanted to take time to extend a special thanks to a number of people who had a large supportive role, and without such help, would have made completion of the book far more difficult. First and foremost, we want to extend a big thank you to Dr. Roger Levine. He was critical in helping us develop and implement the nationwide survey of graduate programs, and freely provided his time and expertise in analysis of the massive data we received from the survey. We would also like to thank all of the current and former editors at Cambridge University Press (Martin Griffiths, Victoria Parrin, Ilaria Tassistro, and Katrina Halliday) for their help in developing this idea; with a special thanks to former Cambridge University Press editor Martin Griffiths for initially believing in our project idea and for his effort to get the project commissioned. We also want to thank the anonymous domestic and international reviewers of our book proposal. Each reviewer provided a fresh perspective and challenged us to think about how we developed and presented the book in a way that has resulted in what we believe is a great product. We owe a lot of gratitude to Kate Sturdivant Gibson, Esq., who served as our legal advisor free of charge, and helped us navigate the numerous intricacies of contract negotiation and language.

We want to thank Megumi Sutherland (formerly Shimizu) and Catalina Pimiento for providing great background information about international students, and whose initial insights allowed us to develop questions and ideas to ask others to enable a more comprehensive understanding of the perspective of international students regarding graduate application. In that vein, we would also like to thank Steven Baer and Morgan Gopnik for their perspectives about nontraditional students applying to graduate school, the foundation of which allowed us to formulate more official questions to ask a larger body of nontraditional students. We would like to thank Caleb C. McKinney and Lauren Wyatt for their insight into graduate programs that use a lab rotation for matching graduate students with major advisors, and we would also like to thank Lynn Wilking and Cherlynn Clarry for proofreading early drafts of many of the chapters.

We also want to provide a big thanks to Duke University and the National Science Foundation OCE-PRF who provided support to allow Dr. S. Kersey Sturdivant to work on this project. It is important that we acknowledge the Virginia Institute of Marine Science, College of William & Mary (where we both attended graduate school) and our former graduate advisors Drs. Robert Diaz, Rochelle Seitz, and Mark Patterson for our wonderful experience in graduate school, which is where we initially conceived producing this book so many years ago as officemates. We'd also like to thank all of the graduate admissions committees who took part in our survey, allowing for the crucial empirical aspect of this book, rather than relying on our own anecdotal advice, and the graduate students who contributed anecdotes about their graduate application experience. Finally, we want to extend a big thanks to our family and friends who have supported and championed us over the years as we have worked on this book, and motivated us through the highs and lows of putting together such a large, comprehensive, and empirical text, with a special consideration for Dr. Noelle Relles' husband, Aaron Relles.

We thank the following people and graduate programs (those that chose to be listed) for their assistance with this book, either through the advice they provided, anecdotes of their graduate school experience, or participation in surveys from which we derived our empirically based advice:

Roger Levine – Aaron Relles – Martin Griffiths – Victoria Parrin – Ilaria Tassistro – Katrina Halliday – Kate Sturdivant Gibson – Megumi Sutherland – Catalina Pimiento – Steven Baer – Morgan Gopnik – Caleb C. McKinney – Lauren Wyatt – Lynn Wilking – Cherlynn Clarry – Robert Diaz – Mark Patterson – Rochelle Seitz – Iris Anderson – Zach McKelvey – Chris Ward – Tiffany Newman – Andrew Thaler – Jenna Spackeen – Corina Antal – Shelby Rinehart – Savannah Volkoff – Tracy Clarry – Amy Donate – Ryan Huang – Tara Catron – Laura Macaulay – Auriel Fournier – Leah Zullig – National Science Foundation – Southern Fried Science – Nicholas School of the Environment, Duke University – Virginia Institute of Marine Science – College of William & Mary – Department of Biological Sciences, Northern Illinois University – Department of Physics and Astronomy, University of Maine – Department of Chemistry, University of Maine – Department of Chemistry and Chemical Biology, Rensselaer Polytechnic Institute – Department of Ecology and Evolutionary Biology, University of Kansas – Department of Biology, University of Central Florida – Tulane University – University of Nebraska-Lincoln – Department of Biological Sciences, Duquesne University – Department of Biological Sciences, University of Delaware – Biological Sciences, University of Maryland Baltimore County – Department of Chemistry and Biochemistry, The University of Toledo – Department of Biology, University of Iowa – Department of Physics, Ohio State University – Graduate School at Georgia Regents University.

Abbreviations

AAAS	American Association for the Advancement of Science
CA	California
COL	Cost Of Living
CV	Curriculum Vitae
EPA	Environmental Protection Agency
ETS	Educational Testing Service
FY	Fiscal Year
GPA	Grade Point Average
GRE	Graduate Record Examination
GRF	Graduate Research Fellowship
GSA	Graduate Student Association
ID	Identification
IHE	Institute of Higher Education
IELTS	International English Language Testing System
NGO	Non-Governmental Organization
NIH	National Institutes of Health
NOAA	National Oceanic and Atmospheric Administration
NSF	National Science Foundation

NSF GRFP	National Science Foundation Graduate Research Fellowship Program
NSF OCE-PRF	National Science Foundation Ocean Sciences Postdoctoral Research Fellowships
PC	Personal Computer
PI	Principal Investigator
RA	Research Assistantship
REU	Research Experience for Undergraduates
SAT	Scholastic Aptitude Test
SD	Standard Deviation
SUNY	State University of New York
TA	Teaching Assistantship
TOEFL	Test of English as a Foreign Language
TOEFL iBT	Test of English as a Foreign Language Internet-Based Test
TV	Television
URL	Uniform Resource Locator
VA	Virginia

1

Pre-graduate School Preparation

One fish, two fish, red fish, blue fish.
                    – Dr. Seuss, American writer and cartoonist

1.1 Introduction

You may be asking yourself, "What does a Dr. Seuss quote have to do with graduate school application?" When you are an undergraduate you can often feel like you are one insignificant fish in a giant school of fish; especially if you were an undergraduate at a large university. Because of this, and other distractions, it can be hard to get specific instructions on how best to prepare for the next step in your education, that ominous specter known as graduate school. In this chapter, we provide a comprehensive brief of what you should be doing in preparation for graduate school, including the aspects that may seem obvious to some. We also have sections which focus on underrepresented groups, nontraditional students, and international students.

Initial contemplation about applying to graduate school can elicit a wide range of emotions as you ponder the quality of your GPA, prepare for the GRE, and debate whether or not schools will think you are as desirable a candidate as you hope you are! In a traditional sense, graduate education is the final hurdle in committing yourself to a target discipline, and the number of years required to begin fostering expertise in a defined subject can be daunting. That aside, the intricacy of the graduate application process has to be traversed before those concerns can be recognized. Applying to graduate school is a process that can be both difficult and awkward because it involves more than just simple grades; although the application process may deter many potential students, the final acceptance will be rewarding. You can assuage these concerns by positioning yourself with the appropriate amount of preparation before you even begin applying. Although much of this preparation can be conducted while you are still an undergraduate, it can also be continued as a postgraduate, particularly for nontraditional students who may spend some years in employment before returning to school.

1.2 Undergraduate Course Selection

Your undergraduate years can be some of the most defining years in your life. You have just branched out from under the supervision of your parents, and you are free to develop and mature into the person you want to be. Undergraduate education is also a time for you to plan and choose how you want to intellectually stimulate yourself. If you are one of the fortunate undergraduates who recognized early that you want to pursue graduate education in the natural sciences, the courses you choose should reflect that. Few people like Orgo (organic chemistry) but it is a rite of passage for science students that you should wear proudly. More importantly, the courses that you select and take as an undergraduate should lay the foundation for your graduate studies.

When contemplating course selections think about where you want to end up in terms of what field of study you would like to pursue. Determine what traits or educational skills you will need if you were in a graduate program in that field (we provide suggestions for how to determine this later in the chapter), and select your courses based on that mentality. If you are unsure of what educational background or traits you would need for a particular program you are interested in, you can talk with your undergraduate academic advisor, reach out to graduate students at your school, or attempt to contact graduate students at a graduate program you would like to enroll in. We suggest reaching out to a graduate student instead of the PI because graduate students will be aware of what educational background would be useful in the program they are currently in, and may be more likely to respond to such an inquiry than the PI. However, do not let the possibility that a PI might not respond discourage you from trying if you so desire.

To provide an example, let's say you are interested in studying deep sea organisms at a Marine Lab; if you emailed one of the students in a lab doing that work, they might suggest that you get some background in genetics as a lot of genetic work is conducted on deep sea vent communities at present, and a background in biostatistical analysis (this is probably useful if you are going to be in any field of the natural sciences). Similarly, if you were interested in studying immunology, a graduate student might suggest you ensure you understand the fundamentals of cellular and molecular biology, and try not to be intimidated by cytokine pathways, antibodies, and cellular signal pathways. Further, make sure you are able to study with an animal model, as this is a necessity in the field of immunology.

These examples were provided to us from former graduate students in each respective program, and they give you a sense of what you could expect to hear back from students you email, but more importantly they show that the descriptive title of the field does not encapsulate the required skills (e.g. needing genetics for deep sea ecology). We also strongly suggest you email more than one student, and be persistent if you do not hear back from the people you contact. The easiest way to locate students in the lab of a PI is to go to the PI's website. Often they have listed on their website which students are in their lab. Sometimes they may have hyperlinks to those students' graduate student websites. If they do not, you can usually note the names of the students in that particular lab, and then locate them on the university's website in the directory. If this proves too difficult, a simple internet search of the student(s) names with the university/institution will generally bring up a graduate web page providing their email contact information.

Of course, as an undergraduate you will have an academic advisor to guide you through course selection, though this advisor may not specialize in your specific interests for graduate education. Typically, the purpose of the academic advisor in undergraduate education is to ensure that you are meeting your requirements for graduation. These advisors can provide sound advice on course selection within your major; however, discussions with students or scientists at programs that you want to enroll in will be more valuable as the individuals will have intimate knowledge of that field and program, as well as the application process.

1.3 Maintaining a Strong GPA

Your grade point average (GPA) is an important parameter of consideration during application to graduate school; it is a value that represents your cumulative academic performance as an undergraduate. The GPA is calculated by taking the number of grade points a student earned in a given period of time and averaging them based on the class workload (indicated by the credits a class is worth). It goes without saying that if you want to pursue graduate education, it is vital to maintain a strong GPA; the GPA is the best representation of your body of academic work as an undergraduate, and graduate schools look at it closely. With all the distractions in college it can be easy to lose focus. We do not have suggestions about how to maintain your focus, which is something you will have to solve on your own. However, when you are selecting courses, it would be prudent to space out your most challenging courses and not take multiple challenging courses in a single semester (if possible). As we suggested above, you should be taking courses that will prepare you for graduate school, but try to avoid arranging too many of your most difficult courses in the same semester. Inevitably there will be courses you inherently perform better in than others. If you can have one or two difficult courses a semester, you will be able to better allocate your time to focus on these classes. In addition to your final GPA, graduate admission offices look at the courses that make up your GPA, and how well you performed in the courses that most closely represent the field of graduate study you are applying for. Graduate programs in the USA rated performance in "in-major" courses as extremely important (rated 4.0 out of 5.0), and the majority of programs noted that performing well in your in-major classes can make up for average performance in non-major courses. This brings us to our next point.

While it is important to maintain a good overall GPA, it is equally, if not even more important, to ensure that you are performing well in your in-major courses. Your performance in courses in your major (generally science and math courses) provides a view of your capacity for science comprehension and application at the graduate level. For example, if you are applying to a physical science program, but you have struggled in calculus, this could be an indication to a graduate school that you might struggle in their program as well. You need to perform to the best of your ability in your in-major courses, especially those with direct applicability for graduate programs in your area of interest. When given the choice between selecting a student with A) a high overall GPA but lower in-major GPA, or B) a lower overall GPA, but exceptionally high in-major GPA, 96% of graduate programs selected student B. This highlights the importance of the in-major GPA for graduate school acceptance. If you have not performed well in a course that you know will be important for graduate programs you intend to apply to, consider retaking the course, or be prepared to explain your performance in the course. A particularly poor performance in a course would necessitate that you include an explanation for the grade in your personal statement (discussed below) or address it during your visit (see Chapter 7: *Visiting and Interviews*). In any course you take, but especially those courses in your major, if you recognize that you might struggle in the course take advantage of any tutoring available at your college. Tutors are often students who excel in that specific discipline and are able to better explain confusing concepts or processes as they have a student's perspective.

If you do not have a good GPA, there are a number of things that you can do to make up for your less-than-stellar performance in coursework. What a low GPA generally represents (to a graduate admissions office), is someone who did not really comprehend the information they were being taught, or someone who lacked a work ethic to do well in the class. If you are a person with a low GPA, you need to dispel both notions in your personal statement and have letters of reference that support you in that pursuit as well; do not hide from your GPA, tackle it head-on. In your personal statement be forthright about your grades not being of the standard or quality that best represents your intellectual aptitude or work ethic. You should then provide reasoning as to why there were extenuating circumstances that contributed to you losing focus as an undergraduate and not performing to the level of which you are capable. Once you have done this you then need to draw upon other strengths in your application, and this is where you need to have properly prepared and positioned yourself to have experiences and qualities to draw on. When US graduate programs were asked what an applicant can do to help compensate for a low GPA, letters of recommendation had the strongest support, followed by establishing a personal relationship with the potential advisor and research experience from an internship.

1.4 Research Experience

Research experience is one of the most important components of undergraduate preparation for graduate school and provides you with a range of positive benefits, including hands-on involvement in actual scientific studies. The best way to learn about research is through experience. Getting this experience as early as possible will familiarize you with the research process and common terminology in your respective discipline, and help you begin to hone skills and learn techniques that will be of use to you later in your graduate career. It also exposes you to the process of developing research ideas and conducting projects to answer scientific questions. Essentially, a history of research indicates that it is likely that you will be able to "hit the ground running" in graduate school, and will require less initial training than a born-again English major who decides upon graduation that they want to investigate the origins of our universe (though, if this is your predilection, go for it!). While gaining this invaluable experience you also have the opportunity to learn about yourself. Through different experiences, you determine what your research interests are and are not. Are you more of a lab warrior, sporting your not-so-white lab coat with pride? Or would you prefer to be outside, with the wind in your hair, and bugs at your ears? Often students surprise themselves about what truly piques their interests after garnering experience with varied research opportunities. Using this experience to narrow down your interests, even slightly, will aid your search for a potential advisor or graduate research program (see Chapter 4: *Choosing a Graduate Program*).

Another benefit of research experience is that it looks great on your *curriculum vitae* (CV). When you apply to graduate school, one of the facets of the application that represents who you are is your CV. It is best to gain as much research-based experience as possible to include on your CV to show that you are familiar with developing scientific questions, and the process of research and data analysis that goes into answering such questions. Also, with respect to your graduate application, having strong research experience can serve as a buffer or counterweight for less stellar aspects of your application (e.g. below-average GPA or GRE scores). The benefits of research experience for your CV and how to set up your CV are discussed in more detail in Chapter 3: *Your Curriculum Vitae (CV)*.

Research experience is also a great avenue for networking within your potential field; both with peers and senior scientists. Your academic peers will be working directly in your lab, office, or building, and this is a great time to begin setting up your scientific network. Establishing social professional relationships with other students is great because your interactions with them can broaden your horizon about other research experiences and opportunities. Also, later in your career you may cross paths with those same peers at scientific conferences, immediately providing you with a social connection. This is especially important for those new to science. Science meetings can be intimidating places, and we discuss this in more detail later in this chapter. Who knows? You may even end up collaborating with some of these people in the not-too-distant future!

More importantly, research experience allows you to begin establishing relationships with senior scientists who are established in your field. This is important because as you continue your scientific career you will find that it is important to have people who are able to speak about your scientific abilities on your behalf. This usually takes place through the writing of reference letters, but can also occur less formally. It is vitally important to have an established scientist who knows you and your research acumen, and is willing to say, "Yes, this person has what it takes to succeed." How important are letter of recommendation writers? Graduate institutions listed them as extremely important in our survey, and this aspect of applying to graduate school received the highest rating (4.2 out of 5.0). Your references also play an important role in securing additional research opportunities where you can establish more scientific relationships. If you continue on this positive feedback route, when you decide to apply to graduate school, you will have a healthy network of established scientists to call on for letters of support. We suggest that you keep in touch with each of the senior scientists you connect with as you continue your progression. They are more likely to agree to write you a letter of reference, and write one that is accurate and meaningful, if they are updated about where you are in your fledgling career. You may even find that the relationship you have with the scientist you worked with evolves into the potential for graduate work!

Generally, research experience can be garnered in one of three ways: through a research-related job, as a research assistant in a lab, or by having an internship. We distinguish research jobs, where an individual works full-time (forty hours plus per week) from a research assistantship, where an individual works in a part-time capacity; these qualitative titles (internship, research assistantship, technician) are meant to provide some order to the hierarchy of

Importance of selected factors in graduate school admission decisions.

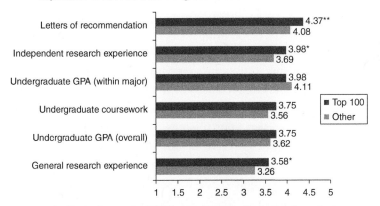

1 = Not important, 2 = Slightly important, 3 = Moderately important,
4 = Very important, 5 = Extremely important
$* = p < 0.05$; $** = p < 0.005$

FIGURE 1.1 A comparison of the most important selected factors in admission decisions between IHEs in the top 100 (dark gray) and IHEs not in the top 100 represented as "Other" (light gray). Asterisks represent significant differences between groups (i.e. Top 100 and Other).

scientific research experience. The research-related job is the most straightforward and can occur during your undergraduate years, or immediately following them. Most research-related jobs occur in a research lab, usually as a technician though sometimes as a lab manager. As a technician you will not have much independent authority (except maybe over undergraduates), but you will get a lot of exposure and "hands-on" experience learning a variety of techniques and methods. Research technician jobs do not generally pay well, but offer a great opportunity to build your scientific skill set, learn new techniques, build your CV, and establish a relationship with a well-known scientist to get a letter of reference (usual this is the scientist leading the lab). Research assistants, another research-related job, tend to have the same style of job as a research technician, though the time they put in is often limited to much less than forty hours a week and is more of a temporary/part-time position.

All research experience is not created equal, and of these three types, often the most valuable research experience you can get is through an internship because it allows you to conduct an independent research project. You can think of independent research internships as mini-modules of what it is like to be an academic scientist. Under the supervision of a PI, from start to finish, these opportunities require you to develop an independent research project, conduct the research, analyze the data, synthesize the results, and present your findings in a presentation and/or paper. When surveyed, graduate institutions stated that research internships where a student conducted an independent research project were very desirable (rated 3.9 out of 5.0), in comparison with general research experience (e.g. technician and research assistantships), which were rated at 3.4 out of 5.0. General research experience is still important, as indicated by the 3.4 value, but it is not as valuable as an internship which provides independent research experience. When research programs look at an applicant, only one of these three research experiences indicates an aptitude to conduct research independently, and this is the internship. We should point out the caveat that often while participating in a research assistantship you may have the opportunity to conduct your own research project. If you do, the quality of that experience is more in line with an internship and should be represented as such in your CV. If you are unable to acquire an internship, but have a research assistantship opportunity, take it! Graduate programs still look favorably upon these experiences, and they hold far greater weight than work experience that is not research related. Graduate programs in our survey rated non-research related work experience as unimportant with a score of 1.7 out of 5.0 (see Figure 1.2).

Research programs are looking for indications that you will be able to operate independently as a graduate student and still maintain a level of success academically and scientifically. When you are in graduate school there will be varying levels of supervision by your major advisor, but there is an expectation of independence for graduate students. When you as an undergraduate are contemplating opportunities to participate in, you need to choose the ones

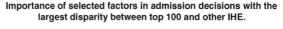

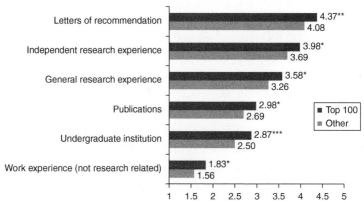

1=Not important, 2=Slightly important, 3=Moderately important,
4=Very important, 5=Extremely important
* = p < 0.05; ** = p < 0.005, *** = p < 0.001

FIGURE 1.2 A comparison of the importance of factors in admission decisions, highlighting those with the largest disparity between IHEs in the top 100 (dark gray) and IHEs not in the top 100 represented as "Other" (light gray). Asterisks represent significant differences between groups (i.e. Top 100 and Other).

that best show you can conduct research independently. It may be fun to go to Latin America and assist in sea turtle restoration, but it is better for you academically to go to a place that will allow you to conduct an independent research project. Further, when participating in internships or research assistantships that do not inherently have an independent research project built into their program, request the opportunity to develop an independent research project in conjunction with whatever work you may be participating in.

If you are feeling confident about requesting the opportunity to conduct an independent research project, there are a number of ways to approach this subject. Before you begin your research experience, you can talk with your supervisor (usually this will be your PI) about the possibility for developing an independent research project. When doing so, express your desire to develop an independent hypothesis (with supervision, of course) and test that hypothesis through experimentation. Explain that you want this experience to assist in your training as a young scientist, and express your desire to potentially use the results from your project to present at a conference or even potentially publish a manuscript. Reassure your PI that this project will not interfere with your work in their lab. If at all possible, you should endeavor to have your independent research project incorporate the work you already have to do for your internship/research assistantship, making the most efficient use of your time. If your supervisor agrees with your request, make sure they commit, or appoint someone senior in their lab, to help you with this endeavor (i.e. hypothesis formulation, project development, etc.). This is not something for the inexperienced, and you are going to want as much help as possible.

1.5 Attending Scientific Conferences

One of the important reasons you want to ensure that you are conducting your own independent research project when you are participating in research experiences is that it provides you with material to present at scientific conferences. In this section we are going to cover what a scientific conference is and why it has importance for acceptance into graduate school.

Science conferences are generally discipline-specific meetings where scientists come together to share the findings from their most recent work. There are generally two formats in which the work is shared, oral and poster presentation. Securing an oral presentation is extremely competitive and is generally reserved for well-formulated research projects with timely and significant results. Oral presentations are divided into sessions with specific focuses, and from morning to early evening concurrent oral sessions take place. Oral sessions generally have an associated poster session, where presenters stand by their posters and conference attendees walk around and engage with the presenters. These two methods, oral and poster sessions, are the main component of conferences, but there are also a number of workshops (many geared toward students), board meetings, and official social activities planned; these are great opportunities to network, which we will touch on later. When you are at a conference, this is a great time to be exposed to a variety of research topics. You should use the oral and poster presentations as an avenue to help you determine your research interests. If you hear a talk and think, "Wow that research was cool!", stay in that session and see what else might pique your interest. As we mentioned earlier, presentations are grouped by research focus, so if you hear something you like there is a high probability that other presentations, although on different research projects, will be of interest to you.

Scientists utilize these meetings to present new findings, socialize, and receive feedback from colleagues about ongoing research projects. Importantly, many PIs also go to meetings to try and recruit new graduate students. A good impetus for your attendance at a conference is to present your work and sit back and wait for the plaudits from the top PIs in your discipline. Ok, maybe we are embellishing a bit. However, when you go to a conference and present your work you accomplish a number of things: 1) You display that you have the ability to start a project and pursue it to completion. In science, completion of a project usually results in a peer-reviewed publication, a task that we do not cover in this book as it is outside the scope of the graduate application process, but presentation of your work at a conference and receiving feedback from other scientists (a form of peer review) is vitally important. You get the experience of presenting and defending your results, and you also show you know how to complete a research project. 2) You have the opportunity to network with a number of research scientists. Conferences conglomerate scientists from diverse backgrounds and disciplines, making it the perfect opportunity for you to engage with such a disparate group of researchers. If you see a presentation that piques your interest, by all means engage the presenter in a conversation. Even if the presenter is not a PI, they can provide insight into their work, their lab, and their specific field. By participating in conversations with a number of people, you can share and discuss your interests, but you have the added benefit of presenting yourself as a capable individual. In-person impressions make a big difference, and the connections you make at a conference could lead to further internship opportunities, or if a PI is impressed with your scientific aptitude they may inquire if you are interested in pursuing graduate study with them; if they don't, you can always ask if they are interested in taking you on as a graduate student. Being proactive rarely hurts!

1.6 Underrepresented Groups

Groups that are typically defined as underrepresented in the sciences are women, and cultures excluding Caucasians and Asians. Diversity in the sciences is an interesting conundrum. Scientists acknowledge the importance of diversity for ecological success and health; however, for years they have ignored the importance of diversity for scientific function. At a functional level, diversity adds a variety of perspectives that aid the elucidation of current challenges in science. On a more abstract level, there is formal evidence that diversity of orientations (e.g. gender and ethnic diversity) can even trump ability in problem-solving; studies have documented how the presence of diverse perspectives in collective problem-solving leads to more innovative solutions. So if you are in an underrepresented group in science, know that your participation and pursuit of a scientific career is not just warranted, but also sorely needed.

Over the years, in the USA the inclusion of women in science has improved, with graduate programs from our survey reporting an average of 45% females in the student body. However, much work still needs to be done to increase minority participation with programs reporting a paltry average of 10%. If you happen to be from one of these traditionally underrepresented groups, you should feel confident in knowing that increasing the participation of underrepresented groups is a focus for many graduate programs. A 2012 survey of 500 graduate admissions offices in the USA found that more than half of the institutions indicated that attracting a diverse applicant pool was a pressing issue.[1] With this knowledge in mind, you should feel confident that when applying to graduate school, despite the traditional demographics of the natural sciences, diversity is valued.

If you come from an underrepresented group and are not an international student (special considerations for international students are discussed below in Section 1.8), your preparation for graduate school will mostly mirror that which was recommended earlier in this chapter. Maintaining a good GPA, scoring well on the GRE, participating in research opportunities, and networking with scientists are all very critical. The biggest difference in graduate school preparation as a member of an underrepresented group is that there are a number of specific opportunities to increase your possibility of acceptance into a graduate program that revolve around funding. This is detailed thoroughly in Section 5.5 *Specific Funding Opportunities for Minority and Women Applicants*, in Chapter 5, but we note it in this chapter to highlight that you still need to position yourself well academically to capitalize on these opportunities.

1.7 Nontraditional Graduate Applicants

A lot of the information provided in this chapter is relevant for graduate applicants who are either still undergraduates or are not far removed from undergraduate education (i.e. they have been postgraduates for less than a year). However, a number of graduate applicants are individuals that take a significant amount of time off after receiving their bachelor's degree. On average, graduate institutions stated that approximately 12% of applicants had finished their undergraduate education more than two years ago, while 25% had finished their undergraduate education one to two years ago. During this time away from school you become established in your career, maybe begin a family, and adjust to

[1] Bell, N. E. (2012). *Findings from the 2012 CGS International Graduate Admissions Survey, Phase I: Applications*. Washington, DC: Council of Graduate Schools.

professional life both financially and socially. One of the biggest challenges of applying to graduate school for nontraditional graduate applicants can be the change in self-image. As one recent nontraditional graduate student at Duke University put it, "One suddenly goes from being a well-paid, respected professional, who had been a colleague and peer to many of the faculty, to being an 'underling.'" You need to be prepared for the financial challenge this brings as well as the social aspects. If you are considering going back to graduate school, you may need to first save money to compensate for the drastic pay-cut you are going to take downgrading to a graduate student stipend. Additionally, you should understand if you are married or otherwise "attached," that your commitment to graduate education will be a shared sacrifice, both financially and emotionally.

There is also the big challenge of academic adjustment. Depending on the time you have spent away from school, your skills in math and science may have waned, or your undergraduate degree may not have been in science and/or math at all. A big first step is getting a handle on your math and science skills; math is particularly important when taking the GRE (see Chapter 2: *Graduate Record Examination (GRE)*). It may have been years since you have used calculus or chemistry, for example, so it might be useful to take remedial undergraduate science and math courses before applying to reaffirm your knowledge. This has multiple benefits: it refreshes or enhances your science and math knowledge, which will most definitely be put to the test during your first year of graduate school when you are taking core courses; it re-familiarizes you with the process of taking and studying for courses; it indirectly prepares you for the GRE; and it boosts your confidence as you become more proficient in science and math.

When preparing for the GRE there may be an initial fear of difficulty at re-mastering old skills (multiple-choice tests, long study hours, etc.); however, you may quickly discover that your work experience has actually made many of these things easier than they were in your early twenties. View your length of time away from college as a bonus instead of a handicap in preparation for your graduate application. Your GRE score may hold more importance because of your time away since your undergraduate education, but again you have a number of experiences that you have garnered through your career that will only add value to your application. Additionally, when contacting potential advisors do not worry about bias because of your age relative to other applicants; you will quickly realize that your life experience, maturity, and skills are viewed as a huge plus! Some students who go straight through undergraduate to graduate school are in a bubble, and potentially have a hard time relating to broader concerns, or having empathy for business interests. Your practical experience can most definitely be an asset.

You may be applying to graduate school in a field in which you already work. In this instance you will have an advantage as you will already have a working relationship with many of the people you want to work with, and will have invaluable experience in your discipline. If you are applying to graduate school for something far removed from your current profession, it is not a death knell. Many graduate applicants get accepted having little to no experience in the field that they are dedicating themselves to study. Advisors and graduate programs fully expect graduate school to be a learning process for the students they accept. Remember that the goal of a potential graduate applicant is to demonstrate to the graduate school admissions office, advisor and/or program that they are the most capable of achieving success as a graduate student (i.e. you are a student who is capable of conducting quality independent research). If you have skills and knowledge in a particular discipline, great! But a lack of either quality does not preclude your acceptance into a program if you have demonstrated potential to be successful.

That being said, if you are applying to graduate school in a field far removed from your profession, you may need to take certain steps to ensure you are accepted. If you have a lack of familiarity with the field you are applying to, you may feel out of touch; to address this we suggest that you study the core sciences and read as many contemporary manuscripts in that field as possible, as this will serve to mentally integrate you into this field. You also should talk to people in the field about what you think you may want to research, and solicit advice about the field or your career direction. Ask pointed questions about how senior scientists in your field chose their specialty, things that they would do again differently if they could, or pitfalls to look out for, etc. The next big step, if you can, is to participate in a lab. Whatever it takes, beg, plead, coerce (maybe not coerce), but get yourself into a lab and get experience! As we discussed earlier, gaining relevant experience is vital to your credibility as an applicant. The person whose lab you volunteer in can then write you a letter of recommendation in the future. Remember, when applying to graduate school you will need recommendation letters. When surveyed, USA graduate institutions overwhelmingly agreed that letters of recommendation hold importance in admissions decisions, and that letters from scientists in the field hold the most sway, reaffirming the importance of practical lab experience in the sciences.

1.8 International Students

If you are applying to graduate school in the USA as an international student, there are a number of considerations you will have to make as an undergraduate and should be aware of. You will be required to take one of the two major English-language tests: the International English Language Testing System (IELTS), which is more widely accepted in Great Britain, Australia, New Zealand, and South Africa; or the Test of English as a Foreign Language (TOEFL), more commonly accepted at US universities. The TOEFL tests four knowledge skills: reading, listening, speaking, and writing, and can take anywhere from two to four hours depending on if the format is paper- or internet-based (the internet version is the longer of the two).

One of the biggest hurdles that most international students face is the language barrier. Even for international students who are fairly proficient in English, if it is not your native language it can often be difficult to communicate in a 'natural way.' Suggestions for solving the issue of language for non-native English speakers is to find someone who is as close to a native English speaker as possible. This might not be easy in some regions and it may be worthwhile to begin your search for an English speaker early in your undergraduate career. The language barrier tends to be the foundation for a number of issues that may arise for international students applying to graduate school in the USA, including: understanding the application instructions, taking the TOEFL test, and communicating with potential advisors. There is also the added pressure of performing well on the essay portion of the GRE; as one international graduate student put it, "There is a sense that if the perception is that your English comprehension is horrible, your chances of acceptance will be really low." In reality this is far from the truth. Graduate programs are well aware that international students may not be strong in English, and are far more accommodating of this fact when analyzing graduate applications from international students than may be expected. You only have to look at all the international students accepted ahead of you; natural science graduate programs are full of international students with a wide range of English proficiency. On average, graduate programs in the USA are composed of approximately 35% international students. While this is true, it goes without saying that, if you are aware that you may want to attend graduate school in the USA, begin working on mastering the English language as soon as possible. Watching American television shows is a good approach to help you understand the language.

When contacting a potential advisor, international students need to be particularly aware of the possibility for non-responsiveness to email inquiries. One professor at the University of Maryland stated, "There is always the worry that the foreign email you receive in less-than-stellar English is just spam." This is a valid concern for potential advisors because, unfortunately for international students, spammers do target researchers at universities and this may affect the response rate. To avoid this unintentional bias, make connections with researchers, in your country or elsewhere, who may have connections with PIs you want to work with in the USA and then you can use these individuals' names when you send your email of inquiry. Also, if you have a website or appear in an article on the web, you can weave this into your email statement, adding veracity to your inquiry. In addition to these tactics, find someone who is a strong English speaker and have them review your email. Your likelihood of getting a response hinges partially on the ability of the potential advisor to comprehend your email and believe that it is credible.

You will not have to worry about applying for a visa until after you have been accepted into graduate school. In order to apply for a USA student visa you must provide proof of acceptance (your acceptance letter) as well as proof of financial support; the proof of financial support is vital. In general, the importance of outside funding cannot be stressed enough when it comes to acceptance into graduate school. As an international student there are funding avenues in the USA that are closed to you (see Chapter 5: *Funding*), but there are also a number of funding opportunities that will be exclusively open to you. If you can secure funding from your government, or a private entity, your application holds significantly more weight. This is true for graduate students everywhere. Do not forget the importance of funding.

Applying to graduate school in the USA is undoubtedly going to be harder than applying to graduate school in your native country because of the potential for language issues, standardized tests (e.g. TOEFL), unfamiliarity with the USA graduate school system, funding issues, etc. However, you should not let these challenges dissuade you from applying. With proper preparation, and by identifying potential areas of difficulty, you will increase your probability of successfully surmounting these issues and achieving your goal of acceptance into graduate school!

Conclusion

There are a number of things that you can do to best position yourself for graduate school acceptance during your formative years as an undergraduate. The earlier you identify that you want to attend graduate school and begin preparing yourself for graduate education, the better. Remember that when applying to graduate school, advisors or admissions programs are looking at potential applicants from a "risk assessment" perspective. They select students on the basis that they have the best probability of success, indicating that the financial and time investment by the advisor, department, or institution is not wasted. You want to be seen as a low-risk applicant, and one way to achieve that perception is to ensure you are as experienced, skilled, and educationally adept as possible!

2

Graduate Record Examination (GRE)

If my future were determined just by my performance on a standardized test, I wouldn't be here. I guarantee you that.

— Michelle Obama, First Lady of the
United States of America (2008–2016)

2.1 Introduction

With many students receiving their undergraduate education at a variety of colleges and universities, and with each of them having varying standards and degrees of difficulty, it is hard to accurately assess a student's potential for postgraduate education among their peers. Standardized tests came about in the early twentieth century in an attempt to provide all candidates with a single assessment from which they could be judged. Nearly all graduate schools in the USA utilize the GRE, developed in 1949, as a method of ascertaining the intellectual merit of a postgraduate student. This standardized test often causes stress for many graduate school applicants, and as Michelle Obama alludes, can be inaccurately viewed as the "be-all and end-all" to their graduate school aspirations. Poor scores on the GRE can possibly deter a potential graduate school applicant and, alternatively, high scores may give false hope. Are current perceptions of the GRE accurate? How much weight do modern graduate schools place on the GRE in comparison with other facets of your application? These are important questions that can only be answered by graduate admissions offices and were quantified through our survey of hundreds of graduate admissions offices around the USA.

2.2 The Setup of the GRE

Educational Testing Service (ETS) has a website dedicated specifically to the GRE; see Appendix, source 1). The current model of the GRE, the GRE Revised General Test, has been in existence since 2011; it is generally administered on a computer at a designated testing location, but a paper option is also available. The GRE is set up similar to the SAT, which you likely took as part of your preparation for applying to an undergraduate college; it is divided into verbal reasoning, quantitative reasoning, and an analytical writing section. The entire GRE Revised General Test, if taken on the computer, takes around three hours and forty-five minutes and includes a ten-minute break after taking three of the total six sections. The analytical writing portion of the exam is taken first and includes two separate writing tasks, one based on analyzing an issue and another based on analyzing an argument; you are allotted thirty minutes for each task. The writing is scored out of a total of six points, with half-point increments; the score reported is actually an average of your grades on the two writing tasks. According to ETS's GRE website, the analytical writing section measures the student's ability to:

- articulate complex ideas clearly and effectively
- support ideas with relevant reasons and examples
- examine claims and accompanying evidence
- sustain a well-focused, coherent discussion
- control the elements of standard written English

An important consideration regarding the verbal and quantitative portions of the exam is that they are section-level adaptive, meaning the computer selects the second section based on your performance on the first section. The verbal reasoning portion of the exam is made up of two sections of twenty questions each and includes reading comprehension, text completion and sentence equivalence. You will be allotted thirty minutes for each section, scores range between 130 and 170 points. According to ETS's GRE website, this portion of the exam measures the student's ability to:

- analyze and draw conclusions from discourse; reason from incomplete data; identify author's assumptions and/or perspective; understand multiple levels of meaning, such as literal, figurative, and author's intent
- select important points; distinguish major from minor or relevant points; summarize text; understand the structure of a text
- understand the meanings of words, sentences, and entire texts; understand relationships among words and among concepts
- understand what you read and how you apply your reasoning skills

The quantitative reasoning portion is made up of two sections of twenty questions each and includes arithmetic, algebra, geometry, and data analysis. There are thirty-five minutes allotted for each section and an on-screen calculator is provided for your convenience; scores range between 130 and 170 points. According to ETS's GRE website, this portion of the exam measures the student's ability to:

- interpret and analyze quantitative information
- solve problems using mathematical models
- apply basic mathematical skills and elementary mathematical concepts of arithmetic, algebra, geometry, and data interpretation
- and includes real-life scenarios

The revised GRE General Test gives you the option to go back and change answers to prior questions within each timed section; this is a new feature when compared to the old version of the exam. As the test taker you can tag questions as "Mark" or "Review" so that you can easily navigate back to them. Downloading the *POWERPREP® II* software from the ETS GRE website (see Appendix, source 2) is the best way to experience the structure of the exam and style of the questions.

2.3 Preparing for the GRE

There are numerous resources available for preparing for the GRE, including books (Table 2.1), many of which are accompanied by disks (because the test itself is generally taken on a computer), as well as classes that you can take. You should allow yourself sufficient time to prepare for the GRE. As an undergraduate intending to apply to graduate school, it is a good idea to spend the summer between your junior and senior years studying to take the GRE at the end of the summer or in the fall of your senior year. The reasoning behind this approach is that most students begin to contact graduate programs in the fall of their senior year. As is covered in detail in Section 4.6 *Contacting Potential Advisors* in Chapter 4, graduate programs prefer this timing. Having your GRE scores on-hand is useful when interacting with potential graduate programs and/or major advisors. Additionally, you will want to allow time to retake the exam if you are unhappy with your initial scores before graduate applications are due (see Section 2.8 *Poor GRE Scores and How to Deal With Them*).

TABLE 2.1 List of some of the GRE test preparation resources.

Book Title	Publisher
The Official Guide to the GRE Revised General Test	Educational Testing Service
Manhattan GRE	Manhattan Prep
Barron's GRE	Barron's Educational Series
Cracking the GRE	The Princeton Review
The GRE Test for Dummies	Wiley & Sons, Incorporated
GRE® Premier	Kaplan
Preparation for the GRE Test	McGraw-Hill Education

The ETS GRE website is also a great source for preparing for the GRE and provides registration instructions for taking the exam (see below for instructions on registering). If you are taking the computer-based version of the exam, it is particularly important that you familiarize yourself with the format of the exam on a computer. There is a *Prepare for the Test* section on the ETS's GRE website that includes *POWERPREP® II* software for both Mac and PC users. The *POWERPREP® II* software is completely free and includes sample questions, strategies, tips, and two full-length practice tests. This is very valuable preparation for the GRE because it accustoms you to the style of the exam and the use of the computer in taking it. Specifically, according to ETS's GRE website, the *POWERPREP® II* software helps you to:

- practice taking the test
- understand what's being tested
- get familiar with the test design and various question types
- review scored Analytical Writing responses and reader commentary
- review test-taking strategies
- understand scoring

In the verbal reasoning section, vocabulary can be very important, so you may find traditional study techniques like creating flashcards useful. The quantitative reasoning section of the GRE includes basic math skills; there are free math reviews and math content PDFs on the GRE website, and the test itself includes an on-screen calculator during the math section. There are also GRE resources available for purchase through ETS, including a video series, test preparation book, and a mobile app for studying.

2.4 Registering for the GRE

You have to register for the GRE on the ETS website (see Appendix, source 3). Registering for the GRE will require creating a *My GRE Account* on the website, which will also be used to check your scores after you've taken the exam. The name you use on your account must match your legal identification, which will be required of you on test day. Your *My GRE Account* will also allow you to send your scores as needed after taking the exam. You will then have to select the style of testing, either computer or paper-based, and the location where you want to take it based on country, state, and city. You will then be given a list of testing center locations and addresses, with test dates and availability, so you can set up an appointment based on your own preferences of date, time, and location.

What dates you choose to take the GRE will depend on when your graduate applications are due. If you are an undergraduate who is planning on going straight into graduate school upon completion of your bachelor's degree, we suggest taking the GRE in the summer between your junior and senior years, or in the fall of your senior year at the latest. You may want to add in extra time in case you deem it necessary to retake the GRE due to poor performance (see Section 2.8 *Poor GRE Scores and How to Deal With Them*), which you can avoid through adequate preparation. The same time frame applies if you are a nontraditional student (see Section 2.10 for more specific advice for nontraditional students), in terms of taking the exam within a reasonable amount of time before your graduate applications are due, and allowing yourself time to retake the exam if needed.

When scheduling your GRE test, be sure to check the test fees ($195 at the time this book was published), which can be paid by credit or debit card, as well as PayPal®. Make sure you understand the rescheduling and cancellation policies, as it is unlikely you will be eligible for a refund in the event of cancellation or missing the exam.

2.5 Taking the GRE

Bring proper legal identification to the testing center on the day of your exam and ensure the name on your identification exactly matches the name you used to register for the exam. According to the ETS GRE website, your identification must:

- be an **original** document; photocopied documents are not acceptable
- be **valid**; expired documents (bearing expiration dates that have passed) are not acceptable
- bear your **full name** *exactly* (excluding accents and spaces) as it was when registering for the test

■ include a recent, recognizable **photograph**

■ include your **signature** (the name and signature on the ID document must match)

It is also a good idea to bring your confirmation email with you to the testing center on the day of your exam because it will state the date, time, and location of your testing center. If you are taking the paper-based exam you will need your admission ticket, which will be mailed to you, and several sharpened No. 2 pencils.

Your registration fee includes sending your GRE scores to four graduate institutions (if you want to send your scores to more than four there is an additional cost), so be sure to have a list of these recipients on-hand so that you can provide them on the test day.

You want to be comfortable during your exam, so you should dress appropriately, and in layers, so you can adjust accordingly to the temperature in the testing center. Food and drink is not permitted in the testing area, so be sure to eat ahead of time and bring a snack for afterwards if needed – remember the test takes nearly four hours. Cellular phones and any other electronic devices should not be brought into the testing area.

2.5.1 Computer-based Exam

For the computer-based GRE you should arrive thirty minutes prior to the scheduled start time of your exam. Scrap paper will be provided to you by the testing administrator and collected at the conclusion of your exam. Personal calculators are not permitted or necessary, because an on-screen calculator is provided during the quantitative reasoning section.

An unofficial score for the verbal and quantitative sections of the exam will be immediately available upon completion, and at that time you will have the option of cancelling your scores or sending them to graduate institutions of your choosing, four of which are included in your test fee as your "four free score recipients." Your scores can only be reported to recipients of your choosing and at your request, i.e. you do not have to report scores that you do not feel reflect your best work (see Section 2.8 *Poor*

GRE Scores and How to Deal With Them). Upon completion of the test you will be asked to designate your four free score recipients and to choose the *ScoreSelect* option regarding which scores should be reported, choosing between your most recent scores or all scores. It is important to note that when scores are sent, they are reported in their entirety, meaning you cannot choose to send a previous verbal reasoning score along with a more recent quantitative reasoning score. Sending your scores to more than four recipients costs $27 for each additional recipient at the time this book was published.

2.5.2 Paper-based Exam

You will also need to arrive at the testing center thirty minutes prior to the test if you are taking the paper-based exam. You will need to bring your admissions ticket, which you should have received in the mail, as well as several sharpened No. 2 pencils and an eraser. The test administrator will time the different sections of the test and you are not permitted to switch between sections, but a ten-minute break is given after the writing portion of the exam. You will record all of your answers in the test booklet provided by the administrator and will be provided with a calculator for the quantitative portion of the exam.

If you are taking the paper-based exam, you will designate your four free score recipients when you register, as opposed to at the testing facility on test day. However, you can change which scores and to whom they are reported by using your admission ticket correction stub.

2.6 What Your GRE Score Means

The current version of the GRE Revised General Test is scored in three parts. The verbal and quantitative reasoning sections are each scored between 130 and 170, in one-point increments. The analytical writing section is scored between 0 and 6, in half-point increments. In 2014 the means for the verbal, quantitative, and analytical writing portions of the exam were 150.75, 151.91, and 3.61, respectively, based on over 900,000 examinees.[1]

Keep in mind that your GRE scores are only valid for five years after the testing year in which you were tested (July 1 to June 30); after that time you will have to retake the exam for it to be considered in your graduate application.

2.7 The Impact of Your GRE Score on Getting into Graduate School

It is important to remember that your GRE scores are only one portion of your completed graduate application. When asked about her experience with the GRE, Shelby Rinehart, a joint doctoral student at the University of California Davis and San Diego State University, said it was "Horrible, I am not a great standardized test taker. Honestly, get the minimum score required for your school and move on!" ETS includes the caveat that the two limitations of the GRE are that: 1) it does not measure all of the qualities that are important for predicting success in graduate school and 2) it is an inexact measure. Your GRE scores are used by admissions committees to supplement your undergraduate records, recommendation letters, and other application materials, so do not feel as if all hope for graduate education is lost if you get a less-than-stellar score.

Often graduate programs post mean or median GRE (and GPA) scores for recent incoming classes, or list minimum acceptable GRE (and GPA) scores on their applicant website. This is a good way to determine where your score lies in relation to other successful applicants, and you should take this into account when you organize the list of schools and programs you plan on applying to (see Chapter 4: *Choosing a Graduate Program*). You should certainly aim to be above any minimum score requirements, and being above the mean will put you in a good competitive position.

[1] Educational Testing Service® (2015). Tables 1A–IC (www.ets.org/s/gre/pdf/gre_guide_table1a.pdf).

But, just as having a low GRE score does not guarantee you will not be accepted, a high GRE score does not guarantee acceptance into the graduate program of your choice. Your GRE is just one portion of your application materials, which is only one part of the entire application process. Properly preparing and knowing what the schools you are applying to expect will put you in a good position to compete with other applicants for coveted positions.

2.8 Poor GRE Scores and How to Deal With Them

While your GRE scores are not the "be-all and end-all" of getting into graduate school, it is important that your scores are competitive. The best thing to do if you are unhappy with your scores or they do not exceed the minimum expected of your chosen schools is to retake the exam. You can take the computer-based GRE once every twenty-one days and up to five times in a twelve-month period. The paper-based GRE can be retaken as often as it is offered, but keep in mind that it is offered much less frequently than the computer-based exam. Be sure to allow yourself adequate time to prepare and study before retaking the exam, exposing yourself to practice tests via the *POWERPREP®II* free software available on the ETS website. Additionally, a strong score on a GRE Subject Test (detailed below in Section 2.9) can help compensate for a lower score on the general GRE exam by showcasing your aptitude in a particular subject area.

If you still have low scores on the GRE after retaking the exam, it is even more important that the other portions of your graduate application are as strong as possible, like your GPA, letters of recommendation and research experience. Establishing a relationship with a potential advisor or advisors prior to applying can also be of great help, as you would have an inside advocate for your application despite your low GRE score. Most importantly, do not let a low GRE score dissuade you from applying to graduate school. As one graduate student, Savannah, at Duke University, put it, "The GREs do not accurately represent an individual's ability to succeed in graduate school." And she is right!

You can address your low GRE score in your personal statement or during your interview. If you think your GRE score does not accurately reflect your aptitude for science, state as much, and highlight the other aspects of your body of work that support your assertion (i.e. successful internships, publications, presentation at scientific conferences, research experience, success as an undergraduate, thesis project ideas, etc.). You can even highlight that the ETS acknowledges the deficiency regarding standardized testing. It is very likely that the people you are going to be interacting with during the application process will be scientists. Scientists are generally very rational, so if you present a strong logical argument regarding your low GRE, they are prone to listen. In order to do so, it is important to have good supporting evidence to cite your success or potential for success as a graduate student. You could also strategically hint to your letter of recommendation writers to mention your low GRE score in their letters recommending you, again focusing on your other strengths outside of standardized testing.

In short, do not panic if you get a low GRE score. You can spend time practicing and honing your testing skills and retake it. You can also compensate for a low score by detailing all the other qualities that you have as a student. It may be disappointing to get a low score, but there is a lot you can do, and it really is just one component of many in your graduate school application. Even if your score falls below the minimum score listed on a school's website, we would suggest not letting this dissuade you from applying. You just need to acknowledge that based on those scores you are going to have to be very persuasive with the rest of your body of work, to convince the program that you will be a successful candidate.

2.9 GRE Subject Tests

Some graduate programs may require you to take a GRE Subject Test, which measures your knowledge in a particular area of study. Even if your school(s) of choice do not require GRE Subject Tests, they will usually accept them and they could potentially strengthen your application (if you do well on them). According to the ETS (2015)[2], the subject tests are intended for students who have an undergraduate major or extensive background in one of these seven disciplines:

- Biochemistry, Cell and Molecular Biology
- Biology
- Chemistry
- Literature in English
- Mathematics
- Physics
- Psychology

GRE Subject Tests are only given as paper-based exams, so they are only offered at paper-based testing centers during the months of April, September, and October. The total test time for each subject test is two hours and fifty minutes, but there are no separately timed sections within the test. The tests are scored between 200 and 990 points with 10-point increments. The subject tests in Biochemistry, Cell and Molecular Biology, Biology, and Psychology report subscores on a 20–99 scale, in one-point increments.

You should prepare for the specific subject tests by download-ing a practice book that describes the test and gives a full-length practice exam from the ETS website; a practice book will also be mailed to you when you register for the subject test. Each subject test costs $150 at the time this book was published.

2.10 Specific Advice for Nontraditional Students Taking the GRE

Taking the GRE after spending time away from school can be a daunting endeavor. There is a studious mentality that exists

---

[2] Educational Testing Service© (2015). About the GRE® Subject Tests (www.ets.org/gre/subject/about).

when you are in school that you tend to shift from when you are no longer a student. Depending on what you have spent your time doing since your undergraduate education, you may want to allot more time for studying for the GRE than was initially recommended in the preceding sections. For example, while the quantitative reasoning section is often considered basic math, it may involve concepts you have not been working with recently. You may need to refresh your math skills and familiarize yourself with test-style questions. If you have been out of school for a while, your general study skills may also be rusty, so providing yourself with adequate time to initially prepare, and to retake if necessary, will be particularly important for your success with the GRE. Many students who have taken time off between their undergraduate education and graduate school found preparatory courses useful for their GRE preparation. There are courses offered by companies like Kaplan (see Appendix, source 4) and The Princeton Review (see Appendix, source 5), and there are often in-person and online options to choose from. Taking your time with preparation will help to alleviate any worry and concerns you may have about testing, and as you begin to remaster old concepts and skills your confidence in your testing ability is likely to improve.

2.11 Specific Advice for International Students Taking the GRE

On average, international students make up 33% of the USA graduate student body in the natural sciences, ranging from a low of 1% to over 90% at some institutions. As a result, prospective graduate school applicants from around the world take the GRE, and there are testing centers in more than 160 countries. However, finding a convenient location to take the exam may be a problem for international test-takers in particular. This can also be a particular concern if one of the schools you are applying to requires a GRE Subject Test, which are only offered at certain locations because they are only available as a paper-based test. Megumi Shimizu, an international graduate student at Duke University, shared an experience of having to travel four hours from her home in Okinawa to Tokyo, Japan to take a required GRE Subject Test for one of her graduate applications! What this means is that if you are an international student and are planning to take the GRE to apply to graduate schools in the USA, you need to be prepared for the potential complications associated with taking the GRE as an international student. By planning for these things ahead of time, you can avoid the confusion and stress that occur if you wait until the last minute. You can also take solace in knowing that many other international students are having to overcome the same logistical difficulties!

If English is your second language you may struggle with the verbal reasoning and analytical writing portions of the exam in particular, so we recommend focusing on these sections when preparing for the test. The structure of the GRE also may not reflect the model of education in your home country, which again makes familiarizing yourself with the structure and content of the test even more important for international students.

In addition to the GRE, international applicants are required to take the TOEFL iBT test for graduate study in an English-speaking country. This is a test of your ability to understand English at the university level; like the GRE, the TOEFL test is administered by the ETS, but is done so via the Internet. It evaluates how well you combine your listening, reading, speaking, and writing skills to perform academic tasks. Registration cost for the TOEFL test varies by country, but more information can be found on the ETS website (see Appendix, source 6). When taking the TOEFL test, remember to give yourself plenty of time to prepare. Each portion of the TOEFL test requires in-depth knowledge of the English language; therefore, effective test preparation should span several months. Be creative in your studying approach. Preparing for the TOEFL test does not have to only include class sessions and preparatory books. A number of international students we spoke with pointed out that subtitles in movies helped them hone their understanding of English idioms and how native speakers use the language, bolstering their more standard preparation (e.g. English manuals or listening to a professor/English class). Most importantly, make sure you give yourself enough time to retake the test should you not do as well as expected on the first try. No matter how much you prepare, some unexpected things may still happen when you first take the TOEFL test. There's no limit to how many times you can take the TOEFL test, and you can wait to release your scores until you hit the minimum score requirement set by the school(s) you are interested in.

A final important note regarding the GRE for international students is that it may hold greater importance in your application than it does for domestic students. Because you are applying from a country where the educational structure and system may differ from that in the USA, it might be difficult for admissions offices to accurately gauge the academic work you completed as an undergraduate. For this reason, your performance on this standardized test may have a disproportionately larger influence on your graduate school application than students who are USA citizens. This is not meant to scare you, but is just a point to be aware of regarding the importance of certain application aspects for different applicant groups.

Conclusion

The GRE is a necessary evil of your graduate application. However, with adequate preparation you can put yourself into a competitive position for a coveted graduate position. Numerous resources are available for free and for purchase to familiarize yourself with the test structure and content. Academic measures, such as the GRE, are important for comparing applicants to one another and allow graduate institutions to make difficult decisions about acceptance. Preparing for the GRE is important for all graduate applicants, but may be of particular importance for nontraditional and international students.

Although this test has importance in a graduate's application package, it is not the be-all and end-all. Keep this in mind if you do not score as well as you would have hoped. Remember, the GRE is just one component of your application to graduate school, and is not an accurate reflection of who will and won't be successful in graduate school.

3

Your *Curriculum Vitae* (CV)

Success is where preparation and opportunity meet.
— Bobby Unser, retired American automobile racer

3.1 Introduction

An important concept for postgraduates to be aware of during the graduate school application process is that they are selling themselves, plain and simple. If you acknowledge this truth, and prepare yourself for the opportunity to do so, then, as Unser states, success should follow. This can be easier said than done. As a society, humility is seen as a favorable trait and self-aggrandizement is often viewed as arrogant or narcissistic. As such, many people do not have a lot of experience portraying themselves in an overtly positive manner. In the sciences an effective method to sell yourself is through your *curriculum vitae* (CV), as it provides an opportunity for you to boast about your accomplishments. *Curriculum vitae* is Latin for "the course of my life," and should be just that; your CV should display and explain the experiences and achievements that you have accomplished in life, to date, that make you an attractive candidate. The key wording here is what makes you an *attractive* candidate, and applicants need to be wary of including superfluous information. A carefully constructed

CV provides a window into the professional life of an applicant, and the quality of the CV as a whole, including organization and layout, says as much about the individual as what is written.

Remember, you as the student will be a massive financial and time investment by the advisor, department, and institution. Because of this, when you apply, graduate programs will be assessing you from a "risk" perspective. You want to be seen as a low-risk applicant, and one way to achieve that perception is to demonstrate that you have the necessary tools and skills for science. A well-crafted CV portraying your achievements and experiences is a great way to convey that message.

3.2 Importance of a CV

Most admissions offices receive hundreds of graduate school applications each year. Due to the sheer volume of people applying, these offices need a method to assess realistic candidates for admission. Often admissions offices use a minimum GPA or GRE score (see Chapter 2: *Graduate Record Examination (GRE)*), but even this initial cull of applicants can leave a large applicant pool. Step forward Mr. CV. After whittling down the initial applicant pool based on GPA and GRE scores, an admissions office will then begin to browse applicants' CVs. Additionally, when you first make contact with a potential advisor or a PI (see Chapter 4: *Choosing a Graduate Program*), you should provide your CV to the person in order to give them a complete understanding of your scientific credentials. The CV will play an important role in your acceptance to graduate school and you should therefore take the utmost care in constructing it.

So why are CVs important? A CV displays who you are and what you have done scientifically to date. It provides a list of all of your accomplishments in great detail and is a formal way of presenting your professional life to a potential advisor and graduate admissions office. A well-constructed CV can really make an applicant shine, and likewise, a poor CV can damage an application. Subtle items on your CV, such as providing non-pertinent information (e.g. a job at a pizza place), can provide indications about your level of academic maturity and preparedness for graduate school. As such, we have taken time to outline the *Dos* and *Don'ts* of constructing a CV, with suggestions and tips to make your CV an effective component of your graduate school application. As you read through this chapter we have provided sample CV templates for you to follow along with the text (Figures 3.1 and 3.2). Figure 3.1 may be more relevant for students who are applying to graduate school as undergraduates, whereas Figure 3.2 may be better for nontraditional students who have spent time in the workplace between undergraduate education and applying to graduate school. It is important to note that sections from each sample template apply to both nontraditional and traditional students; these are just provided as examples.

An additional layout format for your CV is provided in Figure 3.3.

3.3 Organizing Your CV

It is important to think carefully about how you format your CV; how you arrange the information can help your CV to be read in its entirety, versus having it quickly scanned and discarded. There are a number of ways to format your CV, and a quick internet search will yield a litany of suggestions. In the end, formatting decisions with respect to font size and design are ultimately up to you. However, there are more formal arrangement strategies that we suggest will increase the quality of your CV as a tool for applying to graduate school (See Figures 3.1, 3.2, and 3.3).

Your CV should start with your personal information at the top, including your name, physical address, and contact information (phone number, email, etc.). These items are universally included as the first items on a CV because they show your identity and allow the reviewer of the CV to easily locate your contact information. Below your personal information you should then include your *Education* history. In this section you want to include all of your post-grade school education, including degrees you are currently working on. At this point in your career, it is not necessary

Full Name (First and Last Name with Middle Initial)

Street Address, City, State, Zip
Phone Number
Email Address

EDUCATION
Date   B.S., University of...
            Focus: Environmental Science
            Magna Cum Laude

Date   A.S., Junior College...
            Focus: Biology

RESEARCH STATEMENT
My research interests center around understanding the effects of...

PROFESSIONAL EXPERIENCE
Date   Lab Technician, University of...
            Description of responsibilities and research outcomes
            (if applicable).
            Advisor/Supervisor

Date   Research Experience for Undergraduates, University of...
            Project Description
            Advisor/Supervisor

PEER-REVIEWED PUBLICATIONS

Date   Author Names. *Article Title.* Journal Title. Page Numbers.

CONFERENCE PRESENTATIONS
Date   Author Names. *Presentation Title.*
            Name of Conference. City, State.

RELEVANT COURSEWORK
Microbiology, Biological Statistics...

RELEVANT SKILLS
ArcGIS 10.0, SigmaPlot...
Date   Name of Award

PROFESSIONAL AFFILIATIONS
Date   Name of Organization
PROFESSIONAL REFERENCES (usually three)
Title and Full Name
Affiliation (University, Laboratory, etc.)
Address
Phone Number
Email Address
Relationship to Applicant

FIGURE 3.1 Sample CV layout for students applying to graduate school. Note the inclusion of relevant undergraduate coursework; this can also be included in a nontraditional student's CV.

Full Name (First and Last Name with Middle Initial)

Street Address, City, State Zip
Phone Number
Email Address

EDUCATION
Date   B.S., University of...

RESEARCH STATEMENT
My research interests center around understanding the effects of...

PROFESSIONAL EXPERIENCE
Date   Job Title
        Employer
        Description of Duties

GRANTS/AWARDS
Date   Name of Award
        Granting Agency/Institution

PROFESSIONAL AFFILIATIONS
Date   Name of Organization

PUBLICATIONS
Date   Author Names. *Article Title*. Journal Title. Page Numbers.

CONFERENCE PRESENTATIONS
Date   Author Names. *Presentation Title*.
        Name of Conference. City, State.

PROFESSIONAL REFERENCES (usually three)

Title and Full Name
Affiliation (University, Laboratory, etc.)
Address
Phone Number
Email Address
Relationship to Applicant

FIGURE 3.2 Sample CV layout for nontraditional students applying to graduate school after a time of employment after earning a bachelor's and/or master's degree.

to include information regarding the high school you attended, but do include an associate's degree and beyond if applicable. If you have more than one item to include in the *Education* section (e.g. an associate's degree, a master's – if you are applying for your doctorate, etc.), be sure to include your most recent item first, and end with your oldest experience. This is known as reverse chrono-logical order, and whenever presenting information in a CV you should use this format. The benefit of reverse chronological order is that for each section your most recent experiences are displayed first. Your most recent experiences are often considered the most pertinent because they provide the closest representation of your present state. For each educational item, include the name of the institution, major(s) and/or minor(s), type of degree (e.g. B.S., B.A., etc.), and the year the degree was (or will be) conferred. We highly recommend that throughout your CV you provide dates and years down the left-hand side for improved readability; this allows the reader to easily view your career chronologically. You should also include any honors you received associated with each degree (e.g. *cum laude*).

After your education section, it is useful to include a brief *Research Statement* of around forty to seventy words. This concise statement is a good method to quickly summarize your research interests, and if written in an astute manner shows that you are focused and knowledgeable about the research area you are applying to work in. It is important that you tailor this statement to fit the program you are applying to for each individual gradu-ate application. Including a "one-size-fits-all" research statement that is not representative of the subject field you are applying for can be detrimental to your application, as it suggests a lack of care in preparation for the application. An example of a concise, well-written research statement is included below:

> *My research interests center around understanding the effects of hypoxia on trophic dynamics and the functional importance of benthos in coastal ecosystems. I am also interested in the significance of biodiversity on ecosystem function, and the effects of global climate change and anthropogenic disturbance on estuarine and coastal processes.*

The next section should include the professional experiences you have participated in to date. This section is often titled *Professional Experience*. In this section, list in reverse

		Full Name
		Physical Address
		Number
		Email
Professional	Date	Institution
Preparation		Bachelors of Science, Honors Degree
		Degree: Environmental Science Focus: Marine Biology
		Summa Cum Laude
Research Interests		*My research interests center around understanding the effects of...*
Professional	Date	**REU** Institution
Experience		Description of responsibilities and research outcomes (if applicable).
		Advisor
	Date	**Internship** Organization/Institution
		Description of responsibilities and research outcomes (if applicable).
		Advisor
	Date	**Research Asst.** Institution
		Description of responsibilities and research outcomes (if applicable).
		Advisor
Peer-reviewed		**Your Name**, Co-author names (*Date of Publication*) Title of article. Journal
Publications		Name.
		Lead PI Name, **Your Name**, Co-author names (*Date of Publication*) Title of article. Journal Name.
Conference	Date	**Your Name**, Co-author names
Presentations		*Title of presentation.*
		Name of Conference
	Date	**Your Name**, Co-author names
		Title of presentation.
		Name of Conference
		Relevant Skills Insert skills (e.g., ArcGIS, R Statistical Software...)

FIGURE 3.3 Sample CV using a different layout than that in Figures 3.1 or 3. 2.

	Relevant Coursework	Insert coursework (e.g., Microbiology, Biological Statistics...)
Organizations &	Date	Name of Organization
Affiliations	Date	Name of Organization
Honors &	Date	Name of Award
Awards	Date	Name of Award
References		Title and Full Name
		Affiliation (University, Laboratory, etc.)
		Address
		Phone Number
		Email Address
		Relationship to Applicant

RESEARCH STATEMENT
My research interests center around understanding the effects of...

RESEARCH EXPERIENCE
Date   Job Title
        Employer
        Description of Duties

TEACHING EXPERIENCE
Date   Teaching Assistant, University of...
        Course Name
        Course Description

PUBLICATIONS
Date   Author Names. *Article Title.* Journal Title. Page Numbers.

FIGURE 3.4 Subsample of a CV showing how to separate your Professional Experience section into Research Experience and Teaching Experience sections.

chronological order any scientific-related jobs, internships, research assistantships (RA), or teaching assistantships that you have had. Depending on the extent of your professional experiences it might be useful to create two different sections addressing research and teaching experiences separately. In this instance, your *Professional Experience* section would instead be divided into separately titled *Research Experience* and *Teaching Experience* sections (Figure 3.4). For each item of experience that you add, include: the date that you were in the position; the title of the position; the company, business or institution;

and a brief synopsis of your duties and achievements. If you are listing an internship or a RA, you should include the name of the PI. When adding items to the *Professional Experience* section, it is not advisable to include items that are irrelevant to science. Listing that you worked at a grocery store or a dance studio can make your CV appear unprofessional and amateur. Our assessment of USA graduate admissions programs found that non-science related experiences add little to no value to your application (see Figure 1.2). If you are concerned about whether an item is acceptable to add to a CV, you can consult with your academic or research advisor. If you are no longer an undergraduate, try and ask someone in the scientific field (e.g. a former mentor or peer in science).

To increase your competitiveness as a graduate school applicant, you need to have relevant items in your *Professional Experience* section. Information about your professional experience gives readers of your CV a sense of your scientific exposure and practice, and can imply how serious you are about pursuing a scientific career. Remember that as an applicant you want to be decreasing your risk potential, and a healthy *Professional Experience* section does that by demonstrating that you have what it takes to succeed in a field of research. For undergraduates this section will include internships and research assistantships. For nontraditional graduate students (those individuals that are a number of years removed from having earned their bachelor's degrees) this section may also include more traditional jobs (one where a salary/wage is conferred), and include work experience that is not necessarily relevant to science because it provides an account of what you have been doing with your life in the time since you finished your undergraduate education.

Your professional experiences should provide you with qualities and opportunities to strengthen other areas of your CV. By participating in an internship or doing a RA in a laboratory, at the end of your experience you may have a tangible research product that you can potentially present at a scientific conference (discussed in Section 1.5 *Attending Scientific Conferences* in Chapter 1). If you are participating in a research experience where there is no explicit plan to have an end product for you (something you could present or publish), you could inquire if the project can be designed in a manner such that you can have something to present at a conference. Many undergraduate and intern advisors will gladly accommodate this request if possible, and your initiative will make a great impression, one they will likely remember when the time comes to write you a letter of recommendation.

The experience gained from internships and RAs also provides a great opportunity for you to learn new techniques and information, but you should always have at the forefront of your mind, "How can I best maximize this experience for the benefit of my scientific career?" Using your work from internships or RAs to attend scientific conferences is a great strategy. Another benefit of participating in professional opportunities is that it will allow you to begin establishing connections with PIs that you may solicit later for letters of recommendation or as potential graduate advisors (discussed in Section 1.4 *Research Experience* in Chapter 1; Section 4.4 *Finding an Advisor in Your Field(s) of Interest* in Chapter 4; and Section 6.4 *Letters of Recommendation* in Chapter 6).

If you are fortunate enough to participate in a research experience that results in a publication, you should create a *Peer-Reviewed Publications* section for your CV. Even if you are not the first author, you should still include the manuscript in this section, but you must be listed as an author if you are going to include a publication on your CV. The publication(s) should be listed in a format similar to the way manuscripts are cited in the reference section of a journal. Take a look at the references for the manuscript you published, and this will give you a format to follow. Similarly, if your experience allowed you to present at a conference, you should create a section entitled *Conference Presentations*. In this section of your CV you should list all presentations that you have personally presented, even ones where you were not the first author. However, if you are an author on a presentation but did not present, do not include that information in your CV. For items in the *Conference Presentations* section, include the date you gave the presentation (month and year are sufficient), authors' names, presentation title, and conference name. You can and should use the same format that you chose for publications for uniformity. Again, remember to include this information in reverse chronological order. It is impossible to create and fill this section of your CV without participating in or having professional experience; you need to have scientific experiences in order to have the opportunity to attend scientific conferences or publish scientific manuscripts.

Having a *Conference Presentations* section is useful because it shows that you have experience with the synthesis portion of science. In order to present at a scientific conference, you would have participated in a research project, analyzed the results, and synthesized the results into a meaningful end product worthy of presentation to your peers and colleagues. The rewards for those actions are presenting the results at a conference, and potentially a publication. The *Peer-Reviewed Publications* section is generally not expected if you are just completing your undergraduate degree. Advisors in Ph.D.-specific programs that tend to be more selective may expect you to have a publication or two, but for the vast majority of programs this is just seen as a big bonus. To a potential advisor, a student with a publication signifies one of the lowest forms of risk. Part of the reason advisors take on students is so the student can help the advisor further their research interests and agenda. For advisors taking on students, the primary goal after such a large expense of time, energy, and money is that the student publishes their work in a peer-reviewed scientific journal. Publishing a scientific research paper is a challenging endeavor for even veteran researchers, but it is especially so for novice scientists. Your research project is presented in a document, submitted to a journal, and then undergoes peer review (it is reviewed by other scientists who are knowledgeable in your field). Peer review is inherently critical, and if you demonstrate that you already have experience navigating this process (by having a publication when applying), you can greatly increase your chances of acceptance.

The next items or sections to include in your CV can appear in any order, and are not necessarily required, but are listed here to provide ideas of additional items to include. If you are a member of a scientific organization that information should be provided in a *Professional Affiliations* section. For example, if you belong to a scientific society, such as the American Association for the Advancement of Science (AAAS), you would list it here and include dates of membership. Attending conferences is a good way to gain items for this section. Generally when you attend a conference you are provided with a year-long membership to the scientific society that is hosting the meeting, and because you are a student that membership is usually relatively inexpensive. If you have any relevant *Honors and Awards* they should also be included. Awards that recognize your intellectual or scientific aptitude are encouraged as they show you have academic rigor, which is always a positive; it is also a way to distinguish yourself from the "crowd" of graduate applicants.

Finally, you should include up to three *References* at the end of your CV. This can be important at this stage in your career because when you make initial contact with a potential advisor and provide your CV, they may want to quickly check what another person's perspective is of your scientific ability. Having a *References* section provides them with the opportunity to do so. It is also a good way to advertise that you may have some big-name scientists who are willing to vouch for you. In your *References* section, include the name, position, affiliation, and contact information for each of your references; you will also want to include your relationship to the person (i.e. academic advisor, mentor, research advisor). You should include no more than three references. It is also very important to let each person know you are listing them for this purpose and get their approval as well as gauge whether they will give you a strong positive recommendation.

References play an important role in graduate application. In our survey, graduate programs in the USA rated letters of recommendation as the most important part of the graduate application (rated at 4.4 out of 5.0 – the highest score received in our survey), indicating the importance of this aspect of an applicant's graduate package. This indicates that when it comes to assessing graduate applicants, admissions offices and potential advisors place special importance on how peer scientists rate a potential student. Therefore, it is of importance that you not only establish relationships with people who can serve as good reference letter writers, but that you ensure you leave them with a positive reputation following your experience with them.

In your CV you could also include a *Relevant Coursework* section; highlighting relevant courses from your undergraduate education or workshops you attended that enhance a particular skill are useful additions. The courses you have taken as an undergraduate, and your performance in those courses, are displayed on your transcripts; however, you may be sending your CV as a primer to initiate interest in you as a student. During these instances the person may not have immediate access to your transcripts, as transcripts are provided during the official application process. Having a nice concise section in your CV that briefly lists some of the key courses you have taken that enhance your scientific aptitude is useful, especially if you participated in a workshop that would not be listed on your transcripts (e.g. a short course in statistical programming). Remember, you want to show that you are scientifically competent, and providing a history of relevant coursework does this well. You may also want to create a separate section where *Relevant Skills* or any computer programming experience is listed. This is a good place to include certifications you may have, or statistical software packages you have experience using.

3.4 Coping with a Limited CV

This section is meant to provide suggestions for those people who have little to no relevant work to include on their CV, and to act as a cautionary tale for those who still have time to change their situation. As mentioned earlier, it is important to be involved, in some form or capacity, in gaining scientific experience. If you want to apply to graduate school, you have to present yourself as the best available option. The best way to do this is to do well in your coursework, do well on the GRE, and have an excellent CV. Having scientific experience bolsters your CV; however, you may have decided late in your undergraduate career that you want to focus on science, or you may have decided to switch careers. Here we will address how you, as a graduate school applicant, can counter limitations in your CV.

First things first, you have to understand that if you do not have a good CV or if the items on your CV are not scientifically relevant, it will be obvious to the person(s) reviewing it. We state this because you need to be aware that with a limited CV, often the first thought of the reviewer will be, *why?* If that question is left unanswered, there could be serious issues with your potential for acceptance. As was touched on in Chapter 1: *Pre-graduate School Preparation*, regarding a poor GPA or GRE, you can explain the perceived weaknesses of your CV in your personal statement. The personal statement provides an opportunity for you to share who you are, what your interests are, and your vision for your future (see Section 6.5 *Personal Statement* in Chapter 6), but you can also use this document to articulate why you may be deficient in aspects of your CV. For example, if you are applying to work in a genetics program, but have little to no lab experience with genetics, state this, but then explain why this will not be a detriment to your success as a graduate student. Or even better, you could try and arrange to get this experience by offering to show up to your program early (say over the summer), or shadowing in a lab before you arrive at graduate school. If you state your willingness or intentions to resolve one of your weaknesses, it can make you appear motivated to achieve success despite your limitations.

People generally do not point out their weakness to a potential employer for fear that they may self-sabotage their application by doing so. This is a valid concern, and we are not suggesting you overly disclose your shortcomings to a potential graduate program or advisor, but if you have some academic or scientific limitations that are obvious, it is best to address them. The reality is that if you are bad at math, it will be apparent from your GPA and/or GRE score. Do not hide from this fact. Tackle your weaknesses head-on. Because your weaknesses will be evident to an admissions office and your potential major advisor, without explanation they will come to their own conclusions as to the reason(s) for your poor performance in a subject, or your lack of experience or achievements. You have an opportunity in your personal statement to reshape their perceptions about your limitations, and convince them that they will not be a hindrance to your success as a graduate student.

While you can use your personal statement to communicate with the admissions office or a potential major advisor, a secondary route is to speak with potential major advisors in person (or electronically), and convince them of your aptitude for success despite your limited CV. This route is especially useful because it adds a more personal approach. In Chapter 4: *Choosing a Graduate Program*, we go into more detail about choosing a major advisor. Part of choosing an advisor is making initial contact, which may be in person or through an introductory email. After you have introduced yourself, there is usually more of an in-depth discussion about you as a student and scientist. During this portion of communication you should share your CV, which would be a perfect opportunity to bring up any glaring shortcomings in your application. Be prepared to address the reasons for them and how you plan to resolve the areas of weakness in your CV.

If you can convince your potential major advisor that yes, your CV is not ideal, but you are still a worthy candidate, you will have gained a powerful ally in your bid for acceptance into graduate school. This person can now advocate for your acceptance in spite of the shortcomings in your CV. Again, the most important thing to remember with this approach is that you must have a convincing argument. Be realistic with yourself about what your issues are and why they exist, then attempt to develop a credible plan to address the issue or a strong argument to counter it. This level of self-reflection will require you to spend some time critically thinking about your CV, but is a worthwhile exercise. Before you present your argument to your potential major advisor, we suggest you try it out on some of your peers, your undergraduate academic advisor, or one of the people who will serve as a reference letter writer for you. They may even be able to provide you with assistance on how to make your argument stronger, or give you ideas on tactics to boost areas of your CV that are weak.

Another approach is to find an outside ally who holds weight. Having someone advocate for you always puts you in a strong position, especially if that person is someone with stature within the scientific community or knows the person or people in the program to which you are applying. When assessing who is the best person to receive a letter of reference from, in our survey graduate programs in the USA indicated that a scientist the student has worked with on research-related experience would be the best person to give a reference. A positive recommendation from this type of individual could help counter any weaknesses in an application. The best way to meet well-known scientists is by working in their research labs, as an intern or a research assistant.

Our suggestion to you would be to talk with the people you plan to ask for letters of recommendation. Generally people who write these letters for you ask to see your CV and/or the personal statement you are submitting, because this information provides them with a foundation on which to write a letter of recommendation for you. During this communication you can talk to them about a weakness in your CV that you plan on addressing or that needs explaining, and ask them to address it in their letter. For example, let's say you performed poorly on the math section of the GRE, but have decent math grades on your transcript. You could ask your letter writer to highlight this, and maybe even during your internship there was an interaction where you were able to show competency in applied mathematics. Again, the letter writer could highlight this. Based on data from our survey, letters of recommendation are an extremely important component of your graduate school application, and they can be used strategically to bolster your chances of admission. We want to stress that you should not nitpick through your CV to find weaknesses, but if there are some glaring omissions, like a lack of lab experience when applying to work in a program that has heavy laboratory requirements, it is worth addressing. Similarly, if you are transitioning careers, your letters of recommendation will hold even more importance.

While we generally advise avoiding adding things to your CV that are not scientifically relevant, if your CV is void of experiences because you have just recently switched careers, majors, or just did not get any experience as an undergraduate, it may be useful to add some experiences that show characteristics you possess that parallel characteristics indicative of success in the sciences. For example, if you were an English major before you switched to science and had an internship doing a large amount of technical writing or editing, you could include this experience and explain that you gained invaluable experience with technical writing. Technical writing ability is a useful skill in the sciences for obtaining funding through grants and presenting research findings in peer-reviewed scientific journals. Or if you have experience with machine tools and are applying for a lab that does a lot of instrument manipulation or construction, definitely include these experiences on your CV. There are a number of experiences that, while not explicitly scientific, translate well into the sciences, and often it is a judgment call on whether they should be included on your CV. If you are on the fence about whether or not to add something to your CV, ask your academic advisor; if you are no longer in college, try contacting another scientist (other than the one you are applying to work with), and ask their opinion.

Volunteer somewhere. Let's face it, sometimes you need to bolster your CV, and quickly. If the options discussed above are not viable, or you just want to enhance your CV, volunteer. Volunteering is the easiest approach for you to gain experience, because generally the resources needed to support a volunteer are low (i.e. they do not have to pay you), and most places could always use extra assistance, especially if that help is free. The best way to find a place to volunteer is to search for a scientific opportunity in your general vicinity that will allow you to participate in something along the lines of what you are interested in pursuing in your graduate career. The important point to remember is that you want to be doing something meaningful. For example, volunteering at a local aquarium and manning the reception desk will not be useful for your career as a marine scientist and will add little value to your CV. Remember, you are in a time crunch, but need quality experience. The best-case scenario is that you find a research lab or program that is willing to let you get some hands-on experience with actual scientific techniques. This will quickly bolster your skills, add an important experience item to your CV, and also provide you with a contact that you could use for a letter of recommendation.

Having a strong CV showing lots of experience, skills, and achievements is useful when applying to graduate school, but is not a necessity. Remember that most undergraduates do not have very many items on their CV, and if you are switching careers or majors, it is understandable that you would not have a CV full of scientific items. The CV is one component of a graduate application, and while you do want to put the best effort you can into ensuring your CV is of a high quality, realize that there are other facets of your application that can compensate for a limited CV (e.g. GPA, GRE, references, funding, etc.). Also, as we discussed above, keep in mind that there are always things you can do to improve your CV.

If you feel that your CV indicates you are not ready for graduate school, it might be a good idea to postpone applying for a year to get the experience and skills to enhance your application.

3.5 Particular Consideration for International Students Writing Their CV

From our informal survey with international students who were either current or former students in graduate school in the USA, preparation of their CVs followed similar guidelines to American students with a few minor exceptions. You want to highlight your academic and scientific experience, and think about ways to enhance how it is portrayed in your CV. When preparing your CV, if applicable, draw attention to any USA work or internship experience you have had. As highlighted earlier in the chapter, experience counts in graduate school applications. Some programs may say that no experience is required to apply, but the reality is that having work or internship experience will give you an edge, and if that experience exposed you to the US culture, all the better! Also remember when composing your CV you want to follow the American style of composition that was outlined in this chapter. For example, while it might be very common to include a professional photograph of yourself with your CV in China, that's rarely done in the USA. At all times follow the norms of the American CV style outlined and addressed in this chapter as the instructions provided are also wholly applicable to international students.

Conclusion

A CV displays who you are scientifically, and is one of the most specific and detailed documents that you will supply when you are applying to graduate school. This all-encompassing document can be beneficial and allow you to rise to the top of the applicant pool if properly constructed. Because your CV is a tool to display your scientific aptitude, it needs to be as clear as possible. Put the time and effort into developing, arranging, and formatting your CV, and you will reap the rewards. As you continue to progress in your scientific career, continue to refine or sharpen this tool (your CV) to ensure that when it is applied (submitted) it is effective at properly conveying your scientific achievements and ability.

4

Choosing a Graduate Program

The adviser is the primary gatekeeper for the professional self-esteem of the student, the rate of progress toward the degree, and access to future opportunities.
— Dr. Sheila Widnall, past president of the American Association for the Advancement of Science (1988)

4.1 Introduction

As an undergraduate you probably took into consideration a variety of factors when deciding where to apply, and ultimately where to enroll, including an institution's academic reputation and prestige in your assessment. Academic ranking is an important consideration when applying to graduate school, but selecting an academic advisor, or potential advisors (for those applying for programs with lab rotations), is a more critical factor in the graduate application process. As Dr. Widnall asserts, advisors can play a major role in your career trajectory, and the often intimidating, and sometimes awkward, process of securing potential major advisors at multiple graduate institutions is one of the main reasons we chose to write this book.

Amy Donate, who completed her doctorate at Old Dominion University, stated, "My overall experience [in graduate school] was positive, but selecting a good match for [a] mentor was key to my success." Her words couldn't ring more true! Admissions to medical and law school programs are relatively straightforward – the GPA and standardized test scores best indicate the likelihood of securing a spot at a chosen school. However, in natural science graduate programs a relationship with an advisor and a "best fit" with the potential advisor's research interests can be more valuable. In many instances your major advisor will provide the majority of your funding throughout your graduate education, and could be the person who directly advocated for your acceptance into the graduate program. As an applicant, establishing a relationship with a major advisor is not only important, but often imperative in order to achieve acceptance. Talking to potential major advisors, particularly as an undergraduate, can be intimidating, and in this chapter we provide suggestions to ease the process of approaching a major advisor, as well as tips on how to determine that an advisor will be a good match for you.

Graduate programs come in two different "flavors." One involves establishing a relationship with an advisor before applying, and upon acceptance to the program you become a student in that person's lab. The other scenario entails spending your first year of graduate school rotating through different research labs to get a feel for an advisor's research and how the lab operates, and then you decide with the prospective researchers which lab is the best fit for your interests and their needs. This rotation style of choosing a research lab and academic advisor is more commonly associated with programs in the life sciences (e.g. biomedical) but occasionally is present in earth science programs. Throughout this chapter we will discuss both application processes, as they relate to choosing a graduate program.

4.2 Determine Your Interest(s)

The initial component of the graduate application process involves deciding upon your research interests, a crucial factor in deciding where you want to attend graduate school. Your research interests may be specific or broad; both have advantages and disadvantages, depending on the program or researcher you are interested in working with. Some advisors will see broad, unspecified interests as a weakness and a sign of being unfocused, while others appreciate this mentality as it indicates a willingness to work on a variety of different projects. Typically, advisors that prefer specific interests on the part of the prospective graduate student already have funding for ongoing projects they want a student to focus their research on; this can be advantageous because it indicates a reliable source of funding for the near future. This does not mean that there is no room for intellectual creativity if you enter a program with funding for a specific project; what this indicates is that your creativity may be partially constrained to the confines of the project scope (i.e. the discipline of funding). For example, an advisor could have funding to work on climate change in tropical rainforests; therefore, as a student you could develop your individual project studying some aspect of climate change in rainforests, but if you were interested in canopy tree-soil interactions in temperate forests, you should probably seek another advisor.

The scope of the project design and the amount of independent research you undertake can be a function of the advisor, but also depends on whether you will be pursuing a master's or doctorate degree. It is expected that a doctoral student will be more independent and design more aspects of a project on their own, whereas the advisor may have a specific project in mind for a master's student. You should keep this in mind when applying. If you have to develop a project on your own as a master's student, your time as a graduate student will likely take longer than if a project was already in place (assuming all circumstances were equal in both instances). That being said, there are a number of qualities that a student hones when they are required to develop their own research project, including how to formulate a research question, hypothesis development, experimental approach, and data analysis; all skills that will serve you well as you go forward in your scientific career, regardless of whether you stay in academia.

You should have an idea of your general research interests by the time you apply to graduate school. Working in a laboratory or taking part in a Research Experience for Undergraduates (REU) program is a great way to determine your general interests. Do not feel overwhelmed if you do not have a specific idea of what you want to research, or if you have multiple ideas that interest you. This is very common for many people applying to graduate school. Having a number of general interests and applying to work in graduate programs that are vastly different from each other is okay, just as long as you are interested in what you may end up studying and ensure that you tailor your CV and personal statements for individual programs. It is worth noting that despite all your efforts to determine your research interests, there is still a possibility that you could enter a graduate program and realize once you are there that you want to study something entirely different. This is an inherent risk, and is an important reason for completing internships and research assistantships (RAs) as an undergraduate in order to increase the probability that you will be successful in identifying the area(s) of science that interest(s) you (see Chapter 1: *Pre-graduate School Preparation*).

4.3 What is an Advisor?

Your advisor is the person who will be primarily responsible for overseeing your scientific training and maturation. Selecting an appropriate advisor is one of the most challenging and critical aspects of ensuring that you have a positive experience in graduate school. You will spend a significant amount of time learning from this person, and we strongly suggest you select an advisor not just on merit (which is an important consideration), but also one with whom you can have a strong positive relationship. He or she will be critiquing every aspect of your graduate professional life, including coursework throughout your graduate education and your research project, and will serve as your graduate committee chair. Your advisor may also accompany you to field locations, if that is a component of your research, as well as to scientific conferences, at which you will present your ongoing work. If you select an advisor with whom you have an antagonistic relationship, it could make resolving big and small issues difficult. For example, you may have to share uncomfortably close living quarters with your advisor during travel for conferences or fieldwork. Surely you want to spend those awkward moments with someone you can tolerate and hopefully even enjoy being in their company.

While in the majority of programs surveyed, the department or school pays for the graduate student's initial year of funding (stipend plus tuition), the major advisor often takes over this responsibility for subsequent years. As such, you will usually be expected to work in and contribute to their lab on projects outside of your own thesis work. This may sound time consuming, and it can be, but it will also help you acquire knowledge and skills outside of your own project, increase your marketability when seeking employment, enhance your prospects of appearing as a coauthor on peer-reviewed scientific publications, and teach you the invaluable skill of academic multitasking (i.e. balancing multiple research projects).

So what criteria should you look for in an advisor? Well first and foremost, they should have a research focus that interests you. If you are going to dedicate a significant amount of your time to graduate school, you should be interested in the research your advisor (and you) are doing. Second, what is the advisor's personality like? To put it simply, you need to get along with your advisor. As was mentioned earlier, you will be spending a significant amount of time under their auspices, and due to the nature of scientific research, a portion of that time will be challenging as you experience failures, frustration, and obstacles. Your graduate school experience will go much more smoothly if you encounter and overcome these issues with someone you get along with. Next, what is their style of advising? Advisors vary widely in their approach to managing students, due to a number of variables (e.g. personality, beliefs, availability, etc.). Some advisors tend to micromanage, assigning their students projects and meeting with them multiple times a week (and weekend), even to the point of being overbearing at times. At the opposite end of the spectrum are advisors who are essentially absent. They give their students

FIGURE 4.1 Advisor-student interactions. From: www.phdcomics.com, with permission.

space and allow them to define their own research problem, serving only as a source of advice as needed. Neither advising style is necessarily right or wrong, but where your optimal advisor falls on this spectrum depends on your own personality, preference, experience, and confidence as a researcher. The best way to discover a potential advisor's style is by consulting with their former and current graduate students, which can be accomplished via email or in person during your visit (discussed in more detail in Sections 7.6, 7.7, and 7.8 in Chapter 7: *Visiting and Interviews*).

Finally, try to find an advisor who is well-connected. Your advisor will likely be your primary liaison for establishing collaborations in your field, and for finding employment after completion of your graduate degree. You want someone whose influence (via serving as a reference writer) can help open doors in your career in science. A PI who is frequently invited to speak at seminars and conferences, who has a diversity of coauthors on publications, who has a long list of collaborators on their website, and whose work is frequently cited are all positive signs of a well-connected scientist.

4.4 Finding an Advisor in Your Field(s) of Interest

This section is applicable only to those programs where establishing an advisor prior to acceptance is required. Graduate programs requiring lab rotations are discussed further in Section 4.7.

Once you have narrowed down your research interests, a primary literature search is the first step for finding the top researchers on that topic (or topics). When a major advisor is not guiding a student to success, they are conducting research on their own or with other colleagues. Websites such as Science Direct (see Appendix, source 7), or even Google Scholar (see Appendix, source 8), are good sources to begin your search for a PI who works in your area of interest and could one day become your major advisor. Both of these sites allow you to freely browse a plethora of scientific journal articles in a number of disciplines. If your topic returns too many results, try making your search more specific. You will want to browse as many of the articles as possible, focusing on the most recently published ones; remember, you want to find an advisor who is not a dinosaur (i.e. retired)! Reading scientific articles can be laborious, so the abstracts are a great place to start. They provide a synopsis of the research project and major results.

When you find research that you think is interesting, give the article a quick scan. If it is research you would enjoy, the next step is to try and determine which of the authors listed could be potential advisors. A person's inclusion as an author indicates their involvement in the project and interests in the discipline, but not all authors are PIs; authors on papers can be students in the lab, technicians, government employees, or members of private industry. Determining the PI(s) is going to require a bit of investigative work; note that the PI is not always listed as the first author on a scientific paper, and often a project will have multiple PIs. The most practical approach is to use the Internet to search for each author. A PI will usually be based at an academic institution, and will, therefore, have a faculty web page and even a separate lab or research website. A good idea is to make a list that is separated into different research interests with potential PIs listed, noting the institution at which the researchers are based. Making this list in Microsoft Excel® is an efficient approach. We have provided an example using ourselves and a few other esteemed colleagues as a template (see Table 4.1). We should note that if your list of potential advisors includes us, and Newton and Einstein, you might be on the wrong track with your search.

TABLE 4.1 Example template for recording a list of potential major advisors.

Name	Institution	Research Interests	Email
Kersey Sturdivant	Duke University	benthic ecology, coastal disturbance, Wormcam	kersey@duke.edu
Noelle Relles	SUNY Cortland	coral reefs, remote sensing AUVs/ROVs	noelle@cortland.edu
Albert Einstein	Princeton University	theoretical physics, quantum mechanics	smartal@princeton.edu
Isaac Newton	Cambridge University	classical mechanics, planetary motion, optics	sirissac@cambridge.org

You should repeat this process until you have a sufficient list of potential PIs, and then you will need to spend some time deciphering which of the authors are PIs who could serve as a major advisor. If you search for an author's name and you determine that they are a professor at a research institution, look at their list of research interests. If their interests broadly align with the research interests of the paper, then congratulations, you have solved the PI mystery! Go and get yourself a cookie, but do not stop here. There could be another PI listed as an author, as colleagues tend to collaborate. When you rule out an author as a PI, you can remove them from your list such that you end up with a tidy list of research interests and PIs who have recently published research. You can now spend time learning more about these potential advisors by browsing their web pages, news articles, research papers, etc., and get a sense for who you would like to work with. From here you can narrow your list down even more and use it to select where to apply. Keep this list as it will be useful in the future if you end up arranging a visit to meet your prospective advisor. During these visits students need to come prepared, and part of that preparation involves reading your potential advisor's work (discussed in more detail below, and in Chapter 7: *Visiting and Interviews*).

Another useful method for meeting potential advisors conducting research of interest to you is to attend scientific conferences, attendance at which is predicated on the presentation of research results. Scientific conferences are great networking opportunities and provide an avenue to put your name and research interests on display, and to learn about current research topics and the laboratories and PIs associated with them. PIs who are looking for students usually attend scientific meetings and may find potential students who are already active in research (PIs love this!). As described in Section 1.5 *Attending Scientific Conferences* in Chapter 1, sessions at scientific conferences normally correspond to specific research areas, so if the research you are presenting reflects the research you want to continue to pursue through your graduate education you should be sure to attend as many talks and poster sessions in your session as possible. If you see or hear something that piques your interest, you can (and should) speak to the researchers directly, whether they are undergraduates, graduate students, postdoctoral researchers, or PIs on the project. Any of these people can let you know about ongoing and upcoming research in their labs and put you in touch with the PI on the project(s).

Conferences also generally offer a number of networking events, including lunchtime workshops and seminars, poster sessions, field trips, and evening social activities where mingling is expected and encouraged. These are great opportunities to speak to researchers, potential advisors, and some advisees in a less intimidating setting, and to inquire about future graduate opportunities and ongoing projects in a more informal way. Having your contact information with name and email on-hand is extremely useful in these situations, so you might think about investing in some business cards that you can easily give to any potential researchers; personal business cards can easily be printed at any office supply store or ordered online. On your business card you should consider including the institution where you are currently located, whether you are an undergraduate or employed somewhere, in addition to your name, email address, and phone number.

Although a researcher is less likely to contact you than you are to contact them, giving them a copy of your business card will encourage them to give their card to you, and opening the lines of communication at a conference can give you a starting point to discuss opportunities in their lab. It is also always good to meet with current students and technicians who work with a potential advisor to see how they feel about working with him/her and to get an idea of how the lab is run and how you might fit into the current lab structure. So during your conversation, ask if any of their students are also attending the conference, and if they would be willing to introduce you to these students.

Another strategy for determining a potential advisor is to carefully examine the National Science Foundation (NSF) and the National Institutes of Health (NIH) websites. These two organizations are the premier funding agencies for research in the natural sciences. Both are large government agencies funded by taxpayer dollars; as a result, they are required to report in detail who receives funding and for what. This presents you with a great opportunity to discover PIs in your area(s) of interest that definitively have money for research, and potentially have money for a graduate student. Typically NSF and NIH grants are of a large magnitude and quite often PIs write in funding for graduate students to conduct work under the umbrella of the grant objective. However, depending on where in the timeline of the grant the PI is, they may have already allocated their graduate student funding. So it is important when looking to keep an eye out for the end-date of the grant. Given the difficulty in obtaining money from these two agencies (due to the stringent peer review), a PI that has NSF or NIH funding is also likely to be well-funded in general and adept at obtaining funding, so even if a grant project for a PI you are interested in is ending in the near future, still contact that PI about potential graduate opportunities. Strategies for using these two websites to find potential advisors are discussed in more detail below.

We focus only on the NSF and the NIH as they are the two main natural science funding organizations in the US, but other agencies (e.g. the Environmental Protection Agency [EPA], the National Oceanic and Atmospheric Administration [NOAA]) also have search portals of funded PIs, and with a little diligence you might also use other government-funded agency websites to source PIs. It is important to note that the following paragraphs describe in detail how to find potential advisors on the NSF and the NIH websites. Because it is a detailed description, reading it works best if you navigate to each respective website and follow along with the search examples provided.

If you are interested in an earth science discipline, you should direct your focus to the NSF. Go to the NSF *Award Search* web page (see Appendix, source 9). The setup at the NSF for searching for awards is relatively simple and straightforward. There is a simple search engine to type in your query. You can make your search as simple or as descriptive as you want. In the following example we search for a simple term, "mollusc". Make sure the *Active Awards* box is checked and not the *Expired Awards* box. Remember, you want only those people who have active funding because you are looking for a prospective advisor with money! After hitting the search button, the search engine will retrieve all current awards related to mollusc research and display them on pages you can scroll through. If you select an award topic/title that is of interest to you, you will be transferred to the award page that will list the PIs, their associated university (i.e. Sponsor), and a more detailed description of their research project (i.e. Abstract). Repeat this process until you have a list of potential PIs in your research area of interest. You can use this strategy to then make contact with one or more of the PIs/Co-PIs of interest. We should note that because we used a broad descriptor (i.e. the term "mollusc"), we received hundreds of responses (290 to be exact) from our initial search. In your search you want to try and be as specific as possible at first, and make your search broader as you go along (e.g. search for "mollusc reproduction in disturbed coastal systems" and then simplify your search in iterative steps until you achieve a satisfying result, or reach a simple term i.e. "mollusc").

If your research interests are in the life sciences, specifically in human health or medicine, you can use the same strategy discussed above for the NIH, though the NIH format for searching is a little more complex. First, go to the NIH *Award Search* web page (see Appendix, source 10). On this page there are a lot of options, but we will walk you through what you need to do to make simple searches. Under the *Research and Organization* section make sure that the *Fiscal Year (FY)* box (located at the upper right area of the page) is showing *Active Projects*. Next, in the *Text Search* section, ensure that the *Text Search (Logic)* is selected for "and", and that the *Search in* section has only *Projects* selected. Once you have accomplished those tasks, you can now type in the *Text Search (Logic)* box for research interests of choice, and then select *SUBMIT QUERY* (located at the top and bottom of the page). Once you search for a subject you will be presented with a number of actively funded projects; you can select projects based on titles of interest to you and will then be taken to a more detailed project page with a PI contact (i.e. Contact PI/Project Leader) and university information (i.e. Awardee Organization) as well as a project abstract. Again, in your search you want to try and be as specific as possible at first, and make your search broader as you go along.

4.5 Know Your Potential Advisor (Before Contacting)

After identifying potential advisors, the first thing you will want to do is read that person's research papers to get an idea of the specific type of work that they do. Reading as much of their research as possible will put you in a good position when you initially contact them, as well as when you get to the interview stage of the application process (see Chapter 7: *Visiting and Interviews*). You will want to appear as knowledgeable as possible about the work that they do and how you and your skill set will contribute to that work. In this competitive age, advisors are looking for students who represent the lowest risk potential, i.e. they want to ensure that the student they bring in will be successful. One way to indicate that you possess the skills and determination for success is to demonstrate due diligence in your interactions with a potential advisor. This can be accomplished by learning as much about the advisor as you can before contacting them.

A great first way to find some general information about your potential advisor is to look at their faculty web page, which will usually contain a picture, some educational background, a list of courses they regularly teach, a description of research interests, a list of ongoing funded projects, and recent publications. Their research interests and funded projects will be of particular importance to you. Are their research interests broad and numerous, or very specific? This will be a good indication of what they might be looking for in a graduate student. Some researchers will think that your broad interests are an advantage because you are willing to work on different projects, organisms, and study various systems, whereas others will want students to have very specific ideas about the graduate research project they intend to pursue. Each PI is different and you can gauge this by the breadth (or lack thereof) of the research statement of the advisor (usually listed on their web page).

Another question to consider is when the currently funded projects end? Remember that the timeline of the funding is relevant for whether you are intending to pursue a master's degree (approximately two to three years in total) or a doctorate (approximately five to seven years), and the time frame of a project may not be listed on the PI's web page, so you may have to inquire about it after you make your initial contact. Is it a project you might be interested in working on? Can you see potential for branching off with a research project of your own from the existing project? This will be an important question that is dependent on your intentions to pursue either a master's or doctorate. The recent publications list is a great place to do your homework and read their most up-to-date peer-reviewed scientific articles; reading these articles will be important if you get to the interview stage of applying to work with that particular researcher.

4.6 Contacting Potential Advisors

When asked about his experience applying to graduate school, Zach McKelvey at the University of California, Santa Barbara said,

"I would say the most awkward part of the application process for me was reaching out to potential advisors and attempting to sell myself as a suitable asset to their lab and program." Contacting PIs can be very intimidating, especially when you are at the beginning of your scientific career. As stated above, a very effective way to make initial contact with potential advisors is exchanging contact information at scientific conferences. Sometimes you will email a researcher you are interested in working with, even one you have previously spoken to in person, and your prospective advisor will not email you back. This is frustrating and you may begin to agonize over emailing them again at the risk of annoying them, but the reality is that most scientists at academic institutions receive dozens of emails on any given day and yours may have been lost in the shuffle. The best approach is to act against your worrying inclination, remain persistent, and send another email! Timing when to send the email is also important. You should think about the college schedule, even if you are not currently an undergraduate. Professors are usually busiest at the beginning and end of semesters. Generally speaking, Monday mornings tend to have the highest volume of emails, making it especially easy for yours to be overlooked. It is best to send an email during the middle of the week, and avoid sending them around any long weekends. If you do not receive a reply in a timely manner (approximately two weeks), do not hesitate to email again; simply state that you are following up on your previous email.

In your email be sure to include your most up-to-date CV (see Chapter 3: *Your Curriculum Vitae (CV)*) as an attachment and write informatively but concisely about your interest in their research and your desire to pursue graduate education with them. You will want to state your name and a bit about your background in terms of education and research experience. You should spend the majority of the email talking about your specific interests in their lab and current projects, and how your background and skills are relevant to contributing to such projects. The more knowledgeable you are of their research and ongoing work, the more impressive you will seem. This is where having read your potential advisor's publications will be especially useful. Be sure to have someone proofread both your email and CV, preferably someone with background knowledge in the subject area.

If you are having trouble receiving an email response, it is very useful to call him or her on their office phone, the number for which will be listed on their faculty web page. Again, be conscious of busy times during the semester, the week, and the day, avoiding first thing in the morning, lunchtime, and close to the end of the day. In addition to mid-week, mid-morning is a good time to contact him or her. Faculty members will often have their office hours posted on their web pages, so you can plan on calling them when you know they will be in the office. Some advisors will prefer this more personal method of contact.

If a program you are applying to requires lab rotations following acceptance and enrollment to determine a potential advisor, there are some important differences in the necessity of, and approach to, emailing a potential advisor during the application process (addressed in detail in the following section).

4.7 Lab Rotations for Choosing an Advisor

There are certain fields of study where a lab rotation style of application/admission to graduate school is common. We have found this to be particularly prevalent in the life sciences (e.g. in the field of biomedical and related sciences). The application process in these cases is more similar to the undergraduate application process, where you choose a school or program and they accept you based mostly on grades (GPA and GRE), as opposed to any type of "fit" with an academic advisor at the institution. You may or may not be placed in a specific department or program, which could affect how freely you rotate through labs of your choosing, and your placement and rotations will depend on availability of positions and funding. As a result of this setup, these PIs may not want to heavily interact with prospective students before their acceptance into the graduate program. As one former graduate student put it:

> *The advice I received from my [undergraduate] professors and advisors was not in accordance to the practices of the field I was switching to. My advisors told me to directly e-mail professors I was interested in working with... However, in Biomedical Sciences, you apply to umbrella programs and rotate in a few labs before joining, which meant that professors do not want to talk to you until you have been accepted into the program.* Corina Antal, University of California, San Diego

Though you do not necessarily need to email advisors if applying to lab-rotation style graduate programs, it might still be useful to send an email expressing your interest; this is especially a good idea if your interests are narrowly focused and the PIs you want to work with are in high demand. You could also contact other members of the lab to determine the funding situation and lab culture. If your interests are broader, it is more reasonable to base your decision on other factors like the school's reputation and location (see Section 4.8 *Location, Location, Location*) or other factors relevant to you and your lifestyle. The strategies for determining a good advisor, discussed in Section 4.6, can still be applied later, following acceptance and enrollment, when making a decision during and after lab rotations.

Generally lab rotations will last throughout the first year, when you will also be focusing heavily on coursework, and at the end of the first academic year you will be expected to choose an advisor and begin working with him or her that summer. During your individual lab rotations, prospective advisors might have you work on a small project or contribute to a project with current lab members and learn new techniques, which may help influence which lab you will prefer to join at the end of your rotation. The number of labs you rotate into can vary widely by school, program, and your own preference, but usually you will only rotate into labs of PIs who have space for a new student and can guarantee your funding for the next few years. The selection process may be informal or more formal depending on the school or program. Though the graduate program provides the initial year of funding in a lab rotation situation, and the student's major advisor then covers the funding, it is always a good idea to think about and practice securing your own funding (see Chapter 5: *Funding*).

One of the major advantages of the lab rotation style is that students have an opportunity to experience a lab before committing. It can be extremely advantageous for a student to try out different labs and find his or her best fit in terms of research, the environment, and their relationship with the advisor and other lab members. Sometimes students end up in situations where they do not get along with their advisor, and this negatively influences their graduate school experience. This can occasionally even lead to a student not completing the degree they initially sought. It is very important to choose an advisor that you are compatible with and can work well with. With lab rotations you experience for a short time what it would be like to work with a potential advisor, making it easier to determine if there are issues that would make your experience as a student in their lab untenable.

4.8 Location, Location, Location

I don't regret my decision, but I wish I would have taken the location into consideration a bit more than I did. Grad school is a long road and ideally you want to be in a location that will make you happy. Jenna Spackeen, the Virginia Institute of Marine Science, College of William & Mary.

Do not underestimate the importance of location. This is going to be a place in which you will be living and calling home for several years of your life, and unlike your undergraduate living experience, you will most likely maintain permanent residence in the location the entire time (i.e. you will not be taking yourself and your belongings home between semesters). It is also unlikely that you will be living in on-campus housing as a graduate student, so you will need to take into account the cost of living; this is an important consideration that is often overlooked (discussed in detail in Section 5.3 *Stipend Positions vs. Non-Stipend Positions* in Chapter 5). You may choose to rent or it might make sense for you to buy a home. You will also need to make a decision about whether or not to have roommates, and that will affect the cost of your living situation as well. At a minimum, you should be sure that you could lead a satisfying life in any city containing a graduate school to which you apply.

Although you are undoubtedly excited to go to graduate school and start the next chapter of your life, you will also want to visit family and friends ... at least occasionally. Therefore, it is also important to factor in the cost (monetarily and time-wise) of traveling home when considering locations. If you have a significant other or a family (i.e. husband/wife and kids) to consider, that will also increase the cost for any trips home during your graduate career. You will also want to think about the job prospects for your significant other at the location of the graduate school you choose, as well as childcare options if needed. Many of these are considerations you will make after applying or being accepted, when you actually visit the school, so they are discussed in more detail in Chapter 7: *Visiting and Interviews*.

Conclusion

Choosing a graduate school in the natural sciences is not like choosing an undergraduate institution. Interpersonal relationships can play a much larger role in your graduate school experience, so choosing an appropriate major advisor is a large part of the application process. Your advisor will guide you through course selections, assist you in varying degrees with your research project that will serve as the foundation for your thesis, and they are likely to provide the majority of your funding throughout your graduate career. They will also generally serve as a counsel and confidant throughout your career. Their selection of you as a student is equally as important as your selection of them as an advisor. You want to be impressive as a prospective student, but you always want to be honest about your own expectations so that neither of you are disappointed in the partnership.

5

Funding

Money won't buy happiness, but it will pay the salaries of a large research staff to study the problem.
— Bill Vaughan, American journalist

5.1 Introduction

Funding, funding, funding! Vaughan hits the nail on the head; funding is the life-blood of science that drives and allows for the intellectual ingenuity of scientific discovery. A scientist's greatest joys and fears revolve around that ominous specter that is funding. What does this mean for the aspiring scientist who is applying to graduate school? It is critical to both recognize and acknowledge the importance of funding. In the modern age of technology it has become far easier to locate funding sources, but the competition for funding resources is also ever-increasing. While not required for acceptance, an applicant that secures funding before they even get to graduate school has sealed themselves a golden ticket, one which will open many doors during their graduate school search.

5.2 Importance of Funding

So why is funding important and what role does it have in graduate school acceptance? Before this question can be properly answered, a bit of background is needed about the funding structure in academia. The structure of graduate student funding in the sciences differs from undergraduate, and even most other graduate-level education programs (e.g. medical, law, or business school). In these other programs, typically you, as the student, bear the financial burden of your education. However, frequently in the natural sciences the costs associated with your graduate education are covered by some entity at the graduate institution. Sometimes it is the PI or major advisor who covers these costs, but the department/program or the institution itself can also provide support. Figure 5.1 shows a breakdown of funding support for natural science graduate students in the USA. In addition to having the financial costs of your education covered, graduate students in the natural sciences also generally receive an annual stipend similar in practice to a traditional wage, though the value of the stipend is typically much less than the salary of a full-time job. The value of a graduate student's stipend varies between a

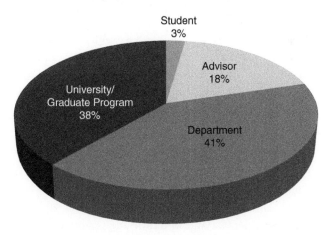

Who pays for a student's first year?

Student
3%

Advisor
18%

Department
41%

University/
Graduate Program
38%

FIGURE 5.1 Breakdown of who pays for a student's first year in graduate school. The figure represents a summary of the results from our survey of ranked graduate admissions programs in the natural sciences (n = 287).

master's and doctorate, with doctoral students earning more (we go into more detail about this in the next section). This model of graduate education is attractive because it removes the financial barrier for students.

When asked about her experience with funding as a graduate student, Tara Raftery said that she "was lucky enough to be funded by a TA [teaching assistantship] during my master's, and an RA [research assistantship] during my Ph.D., which included tuition and a stipend that I was able to live off of. I would not have gone to graduate school if I was unable to secure tuition reimbursement and a salary." Having a system where there are no financial obstructions to education is highly beneficial in that it does not economically prohibit the pursuit of a graduate degree in the natural sciences. If you are motivated and intelligent, you can pursue graduate education in the sciences, and get paid to do so! This method ensures the best and brightest are able to be trained in the sciences, and are able to apply their skills to increasing the state of knowledge in their respective fields.

Money doesn't grow on trees ... even those on college campuses. At this point you may have asked yourself how can this funding arrangement, where students do not pay for their education *and* get paid a stipend, be a remotely sustainable financial model for academic institutions? Taking on a graduate student is definitely a financial investment for both the PI and the academic institution. However, the PI gets a return on that investment through the participation of the graduate student in his or her lab (e.g. fieldwork, lab work, etc.). The hierarchy of academic science is such that academic institutions employ and host PIs. The PIs use that support to bring in funding to conduct research projects in their areas of interest, use grant funding and institutional support to train students, and raise the prestige of an institution with their achievements. The PI provides the graduate student with an avenue to train as a scientist, and in return, the graduate student assists the PI in furthering their academic interests and research focuses; this is where the academic side gets a return on its investment. As a graduate student, in addition to coursework and conducting your own thesis project, you will also be expected to participate in and support research tasks and projects associated with your advisor's work. This broad sweeping directive could involve anything from conducting work in the field, analyzing data, repairing equipment, writing reports, mentoring undergraduates, etc. Fear not, you will not have to paint your PI's house or clean any gutters (hopefully); support of your PI extends only to academically related activities.

As you can see, graduate students are a key cog in the structure and function of academia. As a fledgling graduate student, this arrangement, being paid to receive your graduate education and training as a scientist, may seem like a great setup that heavily leans in your favor. However, during your tenure in graduate school, as your skills and intellectual adeptness increase precipitously, and your pay does not, you will realize that the pendulum of benefit has swung heavily in the direction of the academic institution; the relatively cheap, but talented labor pool from the graduate student body is a big plus for academic intuitions. Overall, the graduate school model is a win-win for academic institutions and PIs, as well as the graduate students they train. In this mutualistic relationship, PIs get productivity from graduate students, and graduate students get training and experience from completing these tasks. Your advisor and the academic institution are invested in your success, both figuratively and literally, and they are therefore motivated to protect their investment.

With this understanding of the role of funding in graduate education, the importance of funding as a potential applicant to graduate school might now be obvious. As was touched on in Chapter 1: *Pre-graduate School Preparation*, and elsewhere in this book, graduate school application is a lot about risk assessment. Admissions offices and/or PIs are assessing you from a risk potential perspective. They select students based on the highest probability of success in an attempt to ensure that the financial and time investment by the advisor, department, and institution is not wasted. To increase your probability for acceptance, you want to be perceived as a low-risk applicant. One way to achieve this perception is to ensure you are as experienced, skilled, and educationally adept as possible (strategies to achieve this and present yourself in this manner were covered in Chapter 1: *Pre-graduate School Preparation*, Chapter 2: *Graduate Record Examination (GRE)*, and Chapter 3: *Your Curriculum Vitae (CV)*). Another way to mitigate for risk is to remove, or at least limit, the financial obligation of the academic institution or PI. This can be achieved by procuring funding extramurally. A student with their own funding is a very attractive candidate for graduate institutions because those students essentially represent a low- to no-cost financial investment, but still provide all the positive qualities that a graduate student brings (highlighted above).

Though funding is important in graduate education, it is important to note that most students accepted into graduate school are accepted without having obtained their own funding. We want to make clear that independently obtaining funding for graduate school before acceptance can only be beneficial, and for most graduate programs a lack of independent funding as an applicant will not be viewed as a negative or weakness in your application. Remember, the graduate school model provides support for students who are accepted. Part of the purpose of this chapter is to relay how bucking the norm and obtaining your own funding can vastly improve your chances for acceptance, and to provide advice on how to achieve this. To obtain funding for graduate education you generally need to have a cohesive idea of your research direction. For admission purposes, 53% of graduate admissions offices surveyed indicated that students having a specific idea of a research project are desirable, and 47% stated it did not matter. That this value is right around half is an indication that graduate programs in the USA realize students have broad research interests and generally do not expect them to have a very specific project in mind. We do not want to diminish the role independent funding can play in your probability of acceptance, but we also do not want to overstate or imply it is a necessity.

This section touches on a very critical topic. Having funding when you are in graduate school, or more importantly, your PI having funding, is very important. This is something you need to take into consideration when applying, covered in more detail in Chapter 4: *Choosing a Graduate Program*. To summarize a bit of Chapter 4, it is acceptable, and often expected, to ask faculty and students at prospective programs about the funding situation. A graduate program that is well-funded will make your life in graduate school much easier. Even within programs there is a dichotomy regarding funding; some PIs are better funded than others, and this impacts the flexibility their students have with research, attending conferences, purchasing equipment, etc.

You also want to know who is responsible for student funding: is it the graduate program, department, or the PI? This is important to determine because it will vary based on the arrangement of your program (i.e. are you accepted into a program and choose an advisor/PI through lab rotations, or do you choose one prior to acceptance?). You should also determine if teaching assistantships (TAs) are available or required. If you find that graduate students are complaining about excessive teaching loads or that they could not work with their first choice advisor due to funding issues, these are points of concern that you will have to evaluate when choosing a graduate program. Ultimately, you can circumvent this issue if you are lucky enough to obtain your own funding (see Section 5.4 *Applying for Fellowships*). Review Chapter 4: *Choosing a Graduate Program* for a more in-depth discussion on the topic of graduate school selection.

5.3 Stipend Positions vs. Non-Stipend Positions

Graduate positions come in two "flavors" in terms of funding: those that receive a stipend and those that do not. As was touched on briefly above, graduate positions *can* be funded, but this does not mean that they all are. Sixty-six percent of the surveyed graduate programs in the USA stated that they fully covered their master's students, and over 95% stated they fully covered their doctoral students. When a graduate program fully funds you as a student, they pay for your tuition and fees, research expenses, and an annual stipend; some graduate programs also cover health benefits. If a graduate student position is not fully funded it is highly unlikely to pay a stipend, but may cover some or part of the other expenses associated with graduate education, such as tuition. What is and is not covered for non-fully funded institutions varies widely by graduate program. Whether or not a graduate program provides a stipend is an important consideration when taking into account where you apply, what degree you want to study for (master's or doctorate), and ultimately where you intend to go.

So just what exactly is a stipend? The stipend graduate students receive is essentially the wage earned for working in the lab of a PI or working as a TA for the school. On paper, students are required to work full-time (forty hours/week), roughly splitting that time between the lab of your advisor, your own research project, and coursework. The stipend is generally paid bi-weekly like a typical wage, but it is not a salary by definition, and because of this distinction the annual amount tends to be low, but on the bright side there are relatively few taxes taken out. By definition, a stipend is paid during a time of learning or training and the institution does not control your work product, i.e. your thesis project, nor do they deduct federal taxes on your behalf; a stipend is like a wage in practice, so the money you receive for your stipend can be used as you please. An appropriate stipend should cover the cost of reasonable housing, utilities, transportation, and food. You should not expect to accrue any significant savings from your stipend, but it should reasonably cover your cost of living.

The amount of money graduate students receive from a stipend is generally determined institutionally, which makes the value of stipends highly variable based on the location of the graduate institution and associated cost of living (COL), the institution itself (some graduate programs pay more than others as a way to attract students), and your funding type (e.g. external graduate fellowships). The value of a stipend from a graduate program located in an area with a high COL tends to be lower than a stipend in an area with a low COL, but the absolute value of both stipends may end up being the same. For example, a $20,000 annual stipend from a school in San Diego, CA would have less value than a $20,000 stipend from a school in Williamsburg, VA. Attending graduate programs in major urban centers may mean that you will live in a smaller space, have more roommates, or have a longer commute than if you enroll in a program at a more rural institution. To compensate, many major urban universities will offer low-cost housing for students. Nerdwallet Inc. has a handy online tool that helps you figure out the COL throughout the USA and could be useful in determining the full value of the stipends offered at your prospective graduate institutions (see Appendix, source 11).

Graduate students who receive fellowships (both "in-house" and externally) tend to get paid more than their graduate student peers; in order to lure a particularly attractive student, a graduate program may offer them an in-house fellowship that increases their base stipend. Generally when this is done the graduate program will also try to throw in other perks as well (e.g. funds for a laptop, research supplies, etc.). Additionally, graduate students who are awarded extramural fellowships (e.g. from the National Science Foundation [NSF] or the National Institutes of Health [NIH] – discussed in more detail in Section 5.4 below) also tend to get paid much more than their fellow students. At the time this book was published, the NSF and the NIH each paid $35,000 annually. Like individual graduate programs, each fellowship program sets the value for the stipend they pay, and as a result the stipends tend to be higher than what most institutions confer.

Due to the high variability of the COL, it is not always guaranteed that your stipend will be enough to cover your living costs. In instances where the stipend provided does not cover the COL, graduate students have to find other avenues to support themselves, and a common method students use to increase their income is to take out an educational loan. The idea of taking out a loan can be distasteful when stipends in graduate school are intended to cover COL. However, because it is difficult to take on another job for additional income, due to the all-encompassing nature of graduate school on graduate students' time, loans are usually the preferred option. On the bright side, your undergraduate loans (if you have any) will be deferred while you are in graduate school. It is also important to note that many graduate institutions prohibit students from having additional jobs as a default, though institutions may make exceptions for students transitioning into career positions or furthering their education while maintaining a current career. Earning extra income from a side job is generally frowned upon (if not prohibited in your contract). This is not done in an elitist fashion, but it is expected that pursuit of graduate education will be your full-time job and non-academic employment that takes away from that focus, and provides little in terms of intellectual training, should be avoided. Regardless of how you supplement your funding, this is a conversation that you need to have with your advisor. They may expect you to work full-time on your research project, while the financial realities of graduate school preclude that level of commitment. Being aware of the variability of stipends is important, and how you factor stipends into your decision on where to go to graduate school is covered in more detail in Chapter 9: *Acceptance and Decision Time.*

In addition to taking into account the value of a stipend with regard to the COL, you will also have to consider whether or not a stipend is even offered. If you are pursuing a doctorate, it is highly unlikely you will encounter a graduate program that does not offer a stipend, but if you are applying to a master's program there is a very real possibility that your program might not offer stipends to master's students. Why is this? Typically the decision of how master's students are funded is made at the program level; this is not a PI-by-PI decision.

Generally, the distinction between stipend and non-stipend master's students comes down to the thesis, but it could also be due to the financial situation of the institution or graduate program. Master's programs that do not require a traditional thesis or only require a thesis-like project tend not to offer a stipend. These programs largely serve the purpose of transitioning students into the private sector or applied sections of government agencies. Generally, non-thesis master's students are loosely associated with a major advisor, which provides a bit of freedom and flexibility in what project they choose to develop, but as a result of not being tethered to a lab they are not administered a stipend. True thesis programs apply a bit more philosophy and theory into the degrees and require students to develop their academic theses more, such that it could (and should) be published in an academic journal. Because these programs require a more rigorous thesis, the students are more closely associated with a lab and a major PI, and perform duties in that lab in addition to developing their thesis. As a result they are paid a stipend for their work in the lab of the PI. Master's stipends are lower than doctoral stipends as a result of where they fall on the hierarchical academic ladder. Even though this book is generally geared toward thesis degrees, it is important to point out the distinction of when and why stipends are typically not awarded, even in relation to non-thesis master's students.

5.4 Applying for Fellowships

Graduate research fellowships (GRFs) are funding opportunities that are generally awarded by government agencies, though also by several private organizations. They cover you, as the student, so they will follow you to whichever school you choose. There are some fellowships that are school-specific, but the vast majority allow you to choose where you pursue your graduate study. We should point out that graduate programs often have their own in-house fellowships that they award to their students, but when discussing GRFs in this book we are explicitly referring to external graduate program fellowships.

In the natural sciences, the organizations that tend to provide the most opportunities for graduate student funding are large government organizations; the two most prevalent are the NSF and the NIH. The NSF and the NIH each generally award 2,000 GRFs annually. The NSF supports fundamental research and education across all non-medical fields of science, mathematics, and technology (including the earth sciences), and the NIH is its counterpart that covers the life sciences. Both of these organizations offer

GRFs that can be applied for before acceptance to graduate school, as well as once you have enrolled. You can find more information about the NSF's GRF (see Appendix, source 12) and NIH's GRF (see Appendix, source 13) online. These GRFs are very competitive; when asked about his funding experience in graduate school, Ryan Huang replied that it was "tough, I applied for the NSF GRFP three times and eventually received it but I had to be supported by the graduate school via TAships for the first two years."

There are also a number of other potential opportunities for funding from non-NSF or -NIH sources. The Fogarty International Center, which focuses on advancing science for global health, has a comprehensive list of non-NIH funding opportunities for the life sciences (see Appendix, source 14). Sources of graduate fellowship funding could also come from the National Oceanic and Atmospheric Administration's GRF (see Appendix, source 15) or from the Environmental Protection Agency (see Appendix, source 16). Applying for extramural funding can be a tedious process but is very useful training that helps you prepare for applying to graduate school. Fellowship deadlines tend to be set earlier than graduate school application deadlines, and the essays, recommendation letters, CV, and other application materials that you prepare can be repurposed for graduate applications (see Chapter 6: *Applying*).

Why should you apply for a GRF? You should apply for a GRF because if you are awarded one, your chances of acceptance into graduate school will drastically increase. Remember, acceptance into graduate school largely hinges on reducing your risk factor. Removing or reducing finances from the equation virtually eliminates the financial risk of accepting you as a student. Further, many programs or PIs require their current students to apply for fellowships. As a potential student, if you can demonstrate you have already done so, you may impress graduate programs with your apparent competence and motivation. The far-reaching impact of securing your own funding makes it worthwhile to apply for funding before acceptance into graduate school, despite the competitiveness of these funding opportunities. Also, once you begin your career as a scientist (even as early as graduate school) you will have to write grants as it is a facet of academia, so learning the process of applying for funding as early as possible can only benefit you in the long run.

You should be aware that GRF applications could be even more in-depth than your graduate application! When applying for an NSF or NIH fellowship, as listed in the request for proposal (which can be viewed by following the links in Appendix, source 12 and source 13), you will need to provide: *Personal Information*; *Education and Other Experience*; *Field(s) of Study*; *Graduate School Information*; *Personal, Relevant Background and Future Goals Statement*; *Graduate Research Plan Statement*; *Eligibility Statement* if applicable; *Transcripts*; and the names and email addresses of three *Reference Letter Writers*. The NSF/NIH will solicit the names you provide to submit a letter of reference for you. The websites also go on to further state, "Applicants should not send extraneous information or materials such as CDs, manuscripts, résumés, medical reports, or news clippings. These items will not be reviewed with an application. No additional information may be provided by links to web pages within the application, except as part of citations in the References Cited section." Basically, you need to avoid sending superfluous information. All of the application information needs to be submitted electronically through an interactive real-time system called FastLane©, which is used by the NSF and the NIH to organize the submissions of grants or fellowships. Some of the non-NSF -NIH fellowships may ask for a GRE Subject Test score in your area of focus (see Chapter 2: *Graduate Record Examination (GRE)*). While graduate schools have application fees (typically $60–$120), there is no cost associated with applying for a fellowship.

The process of applying for grants and fellowships can be tedious, so allot yourself the proper amount of time to compile your application (including time for review and revisions by peers). Contact your recommendation letter writers and start preparing your personal statement early. You also want to take the general GRE and any necessary subject tests early (discussion about the GRE is detailed in Chapter 2: *Graduate Record Examination (GRE)*, but taking it even earlier than suggested in Chapter 2 is advised in the case of applying for a GRF) so that you can retake the test(s) before the GRF deadlines if you are not satisfied with your scores. You will not want to be studying for the GREs, taking your undergraduate classes, and submitting applications simultaneously. We suggest organizing due dates in a spreadsheet; when you are juggling half a dozen deadlines in a single week, you will inevitably forget to send a transcript (or even an entire application) if you are not organized.

You will also want to follow-up with the people you have requested to write your letters of recommendation. As the deadline for each application approaches, sending reminders to your letter writers is a good idea and will be helpful for them and their busy schedules. Most of your letters of recommendation will come from professors; while your application may be the most important thing happening in your life, it may be one item on a long to-do list for them. Faculty members are so notorious for late letters that it is rumored that review committees will wait a week or more for letters to trickle in anyway. Do not count on this and make sure you stay in close contact with your letter of recommendation writers. If you must, add an item to your spreadsheet titled, *Contact Recommenders*, so you do not forget. Again, avoid waiting until the last minute to apply. The rigor involved in crafting and compiling a fellowship application is such that last-minute applications are rarely, if ever, of high enough quality to warrant acceptance.

You should make potential graduate programs and major advisors aware that you are going to apply for an extramural funding opportunity. You want them to know you are thinking about ways to financially cover yourself, and with particular respect to your potential PI, you will want their help. PIs at graduate institutions know how to craft research ideas into funded projects. If they did not, they would not be PIs at research institutions! Applying for one of these positions will require the development of a research direction/theme and you should not let the lack of a clearly cohesive idea deter you. If you have a sense of what you think you might want to do, you can present it to the potential advisor(s) and ask if they are willing to work with you to craft this raw idea into something more sapient. You will be responsible for putting in the time and effort to develop a coherent idea. Approaching a potential advisor and telling them you want to apply for a GRF and you have an idea to work on the disturbance of worms, for example, is not a well thought-out idea, but is a good starting point. If you are struggling to independently develop an idea with depth, or if you have no ideas but still want to apply, you can try talking with the potential PI and ask them for a bit of direction in crafting a research plan. They should be able to point you to scientific papers that may assist you in developing a research direction that aligns closely with what they do.

It is also important to note that the NSF and the NIH fellowships do not hold you to carry out the exact project that you propose, and there is a fair bit of wiggle room to completely change your project if necessary. The proposal is really meant to test your knowledge of your field and ability to express your thoughts clearly. For this reason, if you are struggling to develop a clear and concise research idea, it is probably better to write a proposal about something concrete that you know well (such as an extension of your undergraduate research) rather than the ambitious yet vague project you would really love to work on. If a graduate program you are applying to requires lab rotations during your first year, they may suggest waiting to apply for a GRF. There is some logic to this; students who apply to graduate programs with lab rotations or a similar system are generally covered by the program/department in their first year. While students may have an idea of whom they want to work with, acceptance into a lab is highly dependent on funding and fit, so a GRF application may be more appropriate during the first year of lab rotations when the student is developing a better idea of which PI they will be working with. GRFs require you to provide your research direction, and that is difficult to do without having certainty about who the PI will be that will train you in graduate school.

An important note with regard to the NSF proposals: while graduate schools and most fellowships focus almost entirely on your research potential, the NSF also emphasizes your "broader impacts" on society, which include the direct impact of your proposed project, public outreach efforts, participation in mentoring programs, and even promotion of international collaborations (a complete description is available from the NSF – see Appendix, source 17). Do not overlook these. The ratings sheets (what is generated by proposal reviewers and used by program managers to determine who is funded) for the NSF proposals mention the presence or absence of broader impacts. Even if you submitted a surefire proposal to unify quantum mechanics and general relativity, explain consciousness, and solve three Millennium Problems in one brilliant swoop, but left out references to broader impacts, the NSF would swiftly reject you. If your research is in a non-medical field and is unlikely to directly impact humanity, then you may be terrified at the notion of writing about broader impacts. Fear not! As listed above, broader impacts include public outreach efforts, mentoring, and other activities not directly related to your research, and the NSF will not penalize you for not attempting to save humanity by solving climate change. Given the novelty of writing about your broader impacts and drafting a full-blown NSF project proposal, it can be extremely helpful to begin by looking at a few sample essays and ratings sheets (see Appendix, source 18).

5.5 Specific Funding Opportunities for Minority and Women Applicants

When it comes to funding, there are always specific sets of requirements that an individual must meet in order to qualify for the available funds. You can be excluded (or included) from applying because the funding is for a specific discipline, education level, or even race or gender. Science has been traditionally a Caucasian male-dominated discipline, but in recent years the presence of women and minorities has been growing in the field (demographics of underrepresented groups were discussed in Section 1.6 *Underrepresented Groups* in Chapter 1). In an effort to increase diversity in the sciences, a number of funding opportunities exist solely for these groups, and can be used as a competitive advantage when applying to graduate school. A 2012 survey of 500 graduate admissions offices in the USA found that more than half of the institutions indicated that attracting a diverse applicant pool was a pressing issue,[1] a clear indication of the importance of women and minority graduate applicants.

A quick internet search will yield a number of graduate school funding opportunities solely for minorities or women in the sciences: e.g. National Physical Science Consortium (see Appendix, source 19) or Ford Foundation (see Appendix, source 20). A useful website that lists a number of funding opportunities for minority and female graduate students can be found on the University of California Santa Cruz's Division of Graduate Studies Minority Fellowships website (see Appendix, source 21). It is important to remember that whenever you are looking at funding opportunities, you need to make sure that you can apply to them as a potential graduate school applicant, and do not need to have already been accepted or enrolled in a program. Requirements for an application will vary with each program. If you are unsure if you qualify for a particular fellowship, do not hesitate to email the point of contact listed on the announcement. It is also important to note that website URLs can change or become outdated, which is why we attempted to provide detailed information about the title of each website in the Appendix so you can conduct an internet search and find the location if the URL changes.

5.6 International Applicants

If you are an international student and are looking for funding for graduate school, it can be a more difficult proposition. The majority of funding opportunities that we discuss in this book come from large USA government organizations, most of which require US citizenship in order to apply. There are fellowships available for international students applying to study in the

---

[1] Bell, N. E. (2012). *Findings from the 2012 CGS International Graduate Admissions Survey, Phase I: Applications.* Washington, DC: Council of Graduate Schools.

USA, but they are not necessarily well-advertised and many international students miss the opportunity to apply for them altogether. Before discussing avenues for international student funding, it is important to understand the difference in costs at non-private schools (i.e. state schools) in the USA for state residents vs. non-state residents. For example, a year of tuition and fees at the University of North Carolina Chapel Hill costs around $8,500 for students who live in North Carolina, and around $33,500 for those who are not considered residents of North Carolina (a huge difference). Establishing residency in a state can instantly reduce your ultimate expense, and you should move quickly to determine what is required to establish residency in the state where you are going to graduate school. If the school is private (e.g. Duke University, also in the state of North Carolina), there are usually no cost differences for in-state and out-of-state residents.

Sometimes the country of origin of international students may offer funding support for those who wish to pursue a scientific education abroad. These scholarships are generally offered to students who are interested in pursuing a master's or doctorate, and may require that the students come back to their home country afterwards and apply their skills there. Some countries do not require students to return to their home countries, but request that students actively contribute to the world in a good way; this could be broadly interpreted. The duration of funding is also variable by country and dependent on the degree you pursue. Because each country's policy varies regarding the award of study abroad scholarships, it is best to investigate if your country offers a study abroad scholarship and if it does, to find out the requirements. Similar to other funding opportunities, if your country does offer funding to study abroad, you should make an attempt to access the funding and let potential graduate programs know about the funding opportunity, as it could be an influencing factor in your acceptance. If your country does not offer support, you should begin looking for a fellowship.

Before you do any fellowship searching, it is important to know that you should *never* have to pay to find or apply for fellowships.

If a fellowship search engine or application asks you for payment or other financial information before you can use it, *stay away*. Reputable scholarships never charge to apply, and there are plenty of free search engines. In particular, UniGo's scholarship directory features a search option specific to international students (see Appendix, source 22). One fellowship option for international graduate students is the prestigious Fulbright Fellowship, an international exchange program for graduate-level students with excellent academic records and some work experience (see Appendix, source 23). Fulbrights are similar to NSF and NIH funding in that they are highly competitive, but if you are successfully awarded one, you then have access to a large community of scholars that can serve as a support network.

If you are a native of a Latin American or Caribbean nation, the Organization of American States' Leo. S. Rowe Pan American Fund has a listing of scholarships for graduate education. Starting on page 5 of the web brochure, you can sort the funding opportunities by country (see Appendix, source 24). Additionally, the Aga Khan Foundation is a useful option if you live in one of the seventeen countries (across four continents) that this fellowship serves (see Appendix, source 25; note that awards made through this program are 50% scholarship and 50% loan – you will have to pay part of the award back over time). Finally, if you are a non-US resident, and a female, you can apply for full-time funding from the American Association of University Women (see Appendix, source 26), whose goal is to promote equity in education for women globally.

As you can see, there are a number of funding opportunities for international students, and we have highlighted just a few. You can access Education USA to conduct thorough research on colleges and financial aid opportunities (see Appendix, source 27). We also recommend starting with the International Student Exchange & Study Abroad Resource Center (see Appendix, source 28). This site discusses financing your education, and also offers advice on selecting a USA school based on what the different states are like, and provides information about preparing for your stay in the USA – including information about how to calculate just how much money you will need for the particular area of the country in which you will be living.

Conclusion

Funding is an important and unavoidable aspect of science that should be taken into careful consideration as you apply to graduate school. How funding is distributed to students, whether or not a school offers a stipend, and if your major advisor has funding available are all crucial components of graduate school. However, because funding plays such a vital role in academia, you can use this to your advantage to increase your probability of acceptance. Applying for independent funding opportunities has the potential to give your graduate application a significant edge, and if you are fortunate enough to be awarded one of these graduate fellowships you will most likely have secured yourself acceptance at an institution of your choice. So get out there, search thoroughly for funding, and apply for extramural funding sources!

6

Applying

Success consists of going from failure to failure without loss of enthusiasm.

– Anonymous

6.1 Introduction

This statement embodies academic science, and is applicable to the process of graduate school admission. Applying to graduate school can feel overwhelming; the tedium of the application process itself is an unrivaled step along the path toward graduate school acceptance; perhaps not the hardest step, but one that should be undertaken with care. It is important to consider the costs of application fees when choosing which schools and how many total schools you will be applying to. Careful forethought and preparation can spare a potential applicant some of the unnecessary tedium and expense, if the graduate application process is concisely streamlined. Knowing what you want to do, with whom, and/or where, can be the difference between filling out three applications as opposed to sixteen!

Graduate school admissions offices, for programs in the natural sciences, are looking for students who demonstrate the potential to think critically and scientifically, and who can independently complete a research project from beginning to end. This is best demonstrated through your scientific research experiences, but should also be conveyed in the letters of recommendation and personal statement portion of the application.

This chapter is a description of the graduate application process. It includes a detailed discussion on securing positive letters of recommendation, highlights the importance of choosing letter writers who will be supportive and will represent you in the best way to the graduate programs you hope to be admitted to, and provides strategies to ensure they do so in a timely manner. The content and format of the personal statement is also discussed, as well as any other writing samples that may potentially be required. We also emphasize the importance of taking note of deadlines for the various programs and ensuring the application package is complete.

6.2 How Many Schools Should You Apply To?

While applying to a large number and variety of schools may seem like it will increase your chances of acceptance (i.e. a numbers game), it is not necessarily an advisable strategy for producing high-quality applications and being accepted into the program of your choice (or one that is a good fit for you). This is not to say that with proper planning and sufficient time you cannot successfully submit high-quality applications to a large number of graduate programs, but to caution that without proper planning increased applications could reduce the quality as you would reduce the amount of time you spend on each application. You should apply to as many schools as you see yourself potentially thriving at academically, professionally, and personally. We know individuals who applied to as few as one and as many as fifteen (and potential medical students are known to commonly apply to twenty or more schools), though the average is probably between five and ten.

Reasons to limit the number of schools to which you apply include application fees (typically $60–$120/school), time spent applying, and difficulty scheduling visits come acceptance and decision time (see Chapter 7: *Visiting and Interviews*). Reasons to apply to more schools include increasing the probability that you get in somewhere, increasing the number of schools you get to visit, and allowing for a school you are unsure of to surprise you during a visit. Your own optimum number of schools to apply to will depend on how many schools/programs fit your interests, your pre-application confidence in your admission likelihood and school preferences, your financial status, and your time for and interest in visiting schools. Another consideration when determining your ideal number of schools to apply to is the time and energy needed to contact and create a professional relationship with prospective advisors (see Section 4.6 *Contacting Potential Advisors* in Chapter 4).

6.3 The Application Process

When applying to graduate school, it's best to start early as it can increase your odds of being admitted. Many graduate programs have rolling admissions, which means applications are evaluated as they arrive (rather than all at once after the final deadline). We have included a generalized timeline of the graduate school application process and highlighted when you should complete certain actions (see Table 6.1).

This example schedule is for students who are planning to enter graduate school in the fall of the following year. This is a best-case scenario and the timeline attempts to provide time to craft a great application, resolve unforeseen problems (a lost transcript, a late letter of recommendation writer, etc.), and submit with time to spare.

When you are ready to apply, the first step is to go on the school's website and complete an application. The majority of graduate applications are completed in their entirety online, so you should have all your required materials available before sitting down to complete your application. Most schools have an *Apply* tab or button right on their homepage. It may seem like a

TABLE 6.1 A general guide for your graduate school application timeline.

Graduate School Application Timeline		
Time	**Actions**	**Notes**
May	Begin researching potential graduate programs and take the practice GRE.	Your score on the practice GRE will help you determine how much preparation you'll need for the real deal.
June	Register for the GRE.	This might also be a good time to sign-up for a GRE prep test (we recommend the in-person or online options), depending on how well you performed on the practice test.
July	Request information from graduate programs that interest you. Update CV.	After conducting an in-depth search for graduate programs and major advisors (outlined in Chapter 4), begin to make contact with the programs. Inquire with admissions offices about application details, etc.
August	Take the GRE, begin drafting personal statement, contact potential letter of recommendation writers.	Taking the GRE early provides you with plenty of time to retake it if you are not happy with your score. Additionally, drafting your personal statement early allows for ample feedback and revision.
September	Register for the Nov. GRE Subject Test (if applicable), finalize list of prospective graduate programs, begin making contact with programs/ advisors.	Once you have determined what major advisor(s) and/ or graduate program(s) you are interested in, familiarize yourself with the current research of those major advisors you are interested in. Use this information to begin establishing contact with them or the graduate program.

TABLE 6.1 (*cont.*)

Time	Actions	Notes
October	Request official undergraduate transcripts, and send your letters of recommendation writers supplementary material.	We think it is prudent to get supplementary material (e.g. resume, personal statement, etc.) to your letter writers as early as the summer when you first contact them, but definitely no later than October.
November	Take GRE Subject Test, finalize personal statement, check-in with letter writers, and insure transcripts and GRE scores were sent.	You definitely want to make sure your grades and test scores have been sent. Follow-up with your letter writers and remind them of their commitment. Have someone in your field, and a few of your smart friends, read over your personal statement.
December	Officially submit applications.	Complete and submit all applications, keeping copies of every section for your records. Verify with your letter writers that your recommendations have been sent.
Jan./Feb.	Arrange campus visits.	Work with graduate programs and potential advisors to arrange to visit as many graduate programs as you can.
March/April	Visit campuses.	Remember when visiting to be relatively informed about the work the potential advisor's research focuses on.
May	Celebrate acceptance!	From the programs you've been accepted to, make a decision on which to enroll in.

no-brainer, but be sure to choose graduate application/admission, as opposed to undergraduate. At this point in the process you should know which program you are applying to and have taken the required examinations (see Chapter 2: *Graduate Record Examination (GRE)*); the only thing left to do is apply!

You will want to make note of the application fee for each school or program you are applying to, which can generally be paid electronically when you submit your application.

Most applications will begin with your most basic information; name, address, phone number, etc. The repetition of filling out this information is tedious, but is a necessary evil. After completing the personal information section, you will then be asked to select the specific graduate program, within the university, you are applying to; be sure to know this ahead of time, as well as the specific application requirements of your chosen program. Next you will provide your education history; if you attended several colleges (i.e. a junior college and then a four-year school or transferred during your undergraduate education) you will want to have a list of those schools and the dates attended and degrees conferred. You will also be asked to provide your GPA for each of the schools you attended, so having your transcripts on hand will be useful.

Then you will be asked to list your employment history; this section may be painfully brief, particularly if you are an undergraduate. Resist the temptation to "beef up" this section by listing non-relevant jobs; your application should convey your potential for success as a scientist, not your ability to deliver pizzas (though you may be good at it). Any positions working in a laboratory or on scientific projects are most relevant and should be at the forefront of your application; try to get these experiences as early as possible (see Chapter 1: *Pre-graduate School Preparation*). Graduate admissions offices view Research Experience for Undergraduates (REUs) as another highly valued employment experience when applying to graduate school because they show you have been exposed to application of the scientific method (i.e. you have experience asking a scientific question and conducting a study to answer that question empirically). Other relevant experiences include working as a laboratory technician or as a volunteer in a lab; volunteering is a great way to gain experience if you are unable to secure some of the more competitive paid positions. Some non-science work experience may be appropriate to include; for example, if you worked for all four years of your undergraduate education in the school library this could demonstrate good research and organization skills, valuable traits in the sciences. Part-time summer jobs from high school are less impressive and irrelevant; adding these to your application can make it obvious you are trying to fill your resume. If you are coming directly from undergraduate education, admissions committees understand that if you are in your early twenties you may not have a lot of work experience under your belt, but they do want to see that you have the potential to be successful as a scientist.

Other optional sections on the application that may or may not be relevant to you are languages and honors. If you speak any other languages, you should include them in your application, listing how fluent you are in each. As for honors, you want to list any academic awards or honors you have received. This includes any cum laude honors you will be earning with your degree and making the dean's list. Any honors or awards specifically related to science should be listed here with some explanation of what the award was for and what it entails.

While you will have your GRE test scores sent directly to the schools to which you are applying (see Chapter 2: *Graduate Record Examination (GRE)*), you may also be asked to provide your scores on your application. You will want to be logged into the Educational Testing Service (ETS; see Appendix, source 29) so you have access to your scores and registration information. You will provide the date, and then your scores on the verbal, quantitative, and analytical portions of the GRE, along with your personal registration number, which is provided by the ETS.

You may also be asked on your application whether you want to be considered for financial support or if you already have a funding source; this will include funding you have already been awarded and funding opportunities you have applied for (see

Chapter 5: *Funding*). Acquiring your own funding will make you a particularly attractive candidate, but it is by no means required and you should certainly take advantage of any funding sources potentially available to you at the institutions to which you are applying.

One of the more important aspects of the graduate application is the letters of recommendation. Generally you will be asked to provide contact information for your recommendation letter writers, including their name, address, and email. You might also be asked for a phone number, your relationship to the individual, and/or how long you've known the person. You may have to select which format your letter writer will be submitting their letter in; most will prefer to do so online or via email, but some "old school" professors may prefer snail mail. It is extremely important that you ask your letter writers for permission to list them as references (see below for specific instructions on letters of recommendation). You may also be asked whether or not you waive your right to read your letter of recommendation, and your decision on this will be noted in the email sent to your letter writer, which will ask them to submit a letter for your application. We recommend that you do waive your right so that they will be candid and honest; any fears you may have about them writing something negative should come to light in your initial correspondence with them to discuss their willingness and ability to write a letter for you.

The final part of your application is your statement of purpose or personal statement, which is a "one- or two-page statement [that] states your reasons for undertaking graduate work and explains your academic interests, including their relation to your undergraduate study and professional goals" (taken from Cornell University's graduate application website[1]). This succinctly summarizes the personal statement. A detailed description of what should be included in a personal statement, and how it should be written, is outlined below (see Section 6.5 *Personal Statement*).

[1] Cornell University Graduate School (n.d.). Statements of Purpose (http://gradschool.cornell.edu/admissions/statements-purpose).

Depending on the program you are applying to, you may be required to provide additional writing samples or supplementary materials as well. If you have any published work related to the sciences, you will certainly want to include that in this section. Published science shows that you have experience with scientific study that culminates in a tangible product. The ability to write technically and scientifically is highly valued in graduate school and can be underrepresented by graduate applicants. You may also use an appropriate writing sample from an undergraduate course if it is relevant to science and/or the field to which you are applying, and shows skills that pertain to your planned course of study. Any other supplementary materials will be program-dependent so pay special attention to the application instructions for your specific program to be sure you aren't leaving anything out.

6.4 Letters of Recommendation

Based on our survey, 86% of graduate admissions programs stated that letters of recommendation are a very to extremely important part of the graduate application. When compared to other aspects of the graduate application, a strong letter of recommendation received the strongest support from graduate admissions offices as the best way to compensate for a low GPA or GRE score. While you won't personally prepare this portion of your application, you should take special care to select the best letter writers who will represent you and your interests on your graduate application.

Individuals who would be certain to write you a favorable letter of recommendation might not be the most appropriate letter writer (looking at you here, mother). There are multiple factors to consider when selecting a person to write you a letter of recommendation, and you want to focus on those persons who can best attest to your scientific aptitude. For example, you may have a great rapport with your history professor, and they may write a glowing letter about you, but they would have no credibility as a judge of your research abilities in the natural sciences or your scientific aptitude. Try to focus on selecting letter writers who can judge

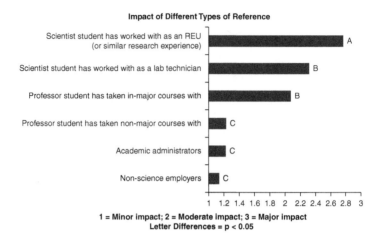

FIGURE 6.1 The impact of different letter writers on a student's application. Letter differences represent significant differences between the factors (p < 0.05).

your potential as a scientist. So whom should you ask to write your letters of recommendation? Ideally, a Nobel Prize winner who swears that you are the spawn of Albert Einstein and Mother Teresa and will revolutionize your field before your qualifying exam. Realistically, at least two PIs or professors who have overseen your research, and an academic advisor who can speak about your coursework, participation in academic programs, and general background and personality. Our survey revealed that graduate admissions offices find scientists you have worked with, either as a lab technician or as an intern, are the best people to procure letters of recommendation from. These people will not only know you as a person and employee; they will know you as a scientist and be able to speak about your aptitude for scientific thinking, and your ability to contribute to and complete a scientific research project.

You may be nervous about asking someone to write a letter of recommendation for you, but rest assured that it is expected and something many scientists consider as part of their job. Setting up a meeting, either virtually or in person, to discuss your graduate goals with potential letter writers is important because this discussion will assist your letter writers in tailoring the contents of their letter to your application and the specific program you are applying to. Being well prepared for even this meeting will ensure your letter writers have an understanding of what you want conveyed, and will increase the likelihood that your letters of recommendation will be of a high quality in terms of content. While a meeting is useful, those who would be writing you a letter of recommendation might be short on time and similar results can be achieved through detailed email correspondence.

Additionally, most letter writers will want your CV and the personal statement you provided (or will provide) to the graduate programs you are applying to, to assist them in crafting their letters. When requesting a letter of recommendation you should also provide the graduate school(s) and specific program(s) you are applying to, including the name of the potential advisor you'd like to work with at each location, if applicable. Include as much detail as possible for each, such as what type of research is conducted at each location and what type of research project you are specifically interested in working on, if applicable. This list will be extremely useful as your letter writer sits down to actually write your letter. When communicating with a letter writer you will also want to discuss your plans for graduate school, including what it was that piqued your interest in this area. Hint: If you can "butter-up" your letter writer by citing them as an inspiration for your future science aspirations, do so, but don't lay it on too thick! You also might want to bring your long-term goals as a scientist into the conversation. For example, do you want to eventually become a PI at an academic institution? The majority of graduate advisors may assume this is your long-term goal. Or do you want to primarily teach at the college-level while engaging undergraduates in smaller research projects? Alternatively, are you interested in a government job in science or a job in the private sector, perhaps doing environmental consulting or working in a pharmaceutical lab? The more detail you can provide to your letter writers, the stronger the endorsement they will be able to give you and they will also be able to speak more specifically about you as an applicant. When a letter writer is specific, it reflects positively about how well they know you and confirms they are qualified to address your aptitude for science and the likelihood of your success in a graduate program.

Most graduate applications require three letters of recommendation; it could be difficult to procure all three from scientists you have worked with in your undergraduate career, especially if you worked for one PI throughout your tenure as an undergraduate. So, who should write your other recommendation letters? If you work in a large research lab you may work more directly under a postdoctoral associate or graduate student who can speak more directly on your skills in science than the PI. You should still ask for a letter of recommendation from the PI, but another scientist in the same lab who oversees your work more directly could provide your second or third letter. Even if you work with this person on a daily basis, you should still set up a more formal meeting to ask them to write you a letter of recommendation and discuss your goals as a scientist; the same amount of preparation should go into this meeting as meeting with a PI.

In most cases you will have the option to have your letter writer submit their letter of recommendation electronically online. This usually involves providing contact information for him or her and checking a box that it will be submitted electronically. At this point your job as an applicant is usually complete and an automated system will send an email to the letter writer asking them to fill out their portion and submit their letter, which will normally be through a link in the email. When they click on the link they will usually have to create an account, which will be linked to your application. The letter writer will not be able to see your entire application, just some basic information like your name, date of birth, and the program to which you are applying. They will then be asked to provide their own basic contact information, like their name, phone number, email, physical address, and the institution with which they are affiliated. In addition to submitting an electronic copy of their letter of support, they will often be asked a series of questions: first about their relationship to you, and then about some of your personal qualities/characteristics; such as your academic performance, your ability to think critically, or your motivation, and their thoughts on your potential for success in a scientific graduate program. When asked to upload their letter of support, there may be specific instructions in terms of formatting that you should make the letter writer aware of in your initial correspondence if at all possible.

You will want to contact your letter writers and start preparing your personal statement early. We recommend contacting potential letter writers during the summer before you apply in the fall. We have found this allows just enough time to hit all of your deadlines in the fall or spring; including obtaining the letters of recommendation you might need for fellowship programs. Be prepared to gently remind your letter writers of approaching deadlines; they *will* forget. You can avoid tardiness from your letter writers by providing them with a friendly reminder (or two).

6.5 Personal Statement

The personal statement portion of the graduate application was rated as moderately to very important by more than 80% of graduate programs surveyed. When drafting your personal statement, keep in mind that there are at least three things that graduate schools want to hear about from you: 1) your interest and motivation for doing research; 2) your experience in and preparation for doing research; and 3) your short- and long-term goals. Your personal statement may also include some background detail on your undergraduate and professional life thus far, paying special attention to what piqued your interest in this particular area of study and the skills you have already acquired that are relevant to this field. Remember the personal statement is your opportunity to sell yourself on your application and insert some of your personality into it.

Your personal statement should display to graduate programs that you are a safe investment. Graduate schools commit a lot of time and money to the students they accept into their programs, and a student who burns out after two years and becomes a Zumba® instructor instead is generally considered a poor investment. For this reason, graduate schools want to know that you have reasons for being interested in research and, ideally, a history of pursuing it. In general, for graduate school applications this is a place where you can be somewhat creative, but in the sciences this is an opportunity to discuss your specific research interests and ideas. The most important factor that graduate programs want to hear about from students in their personal statement is their research interests (Figure 6.2). This is ubiquitous across graduate programs. In our survey of graduate programs in the sciences, we found a fairly even split between programs who prefer specific research ideas and those who prefer more broad interests, so our advice in this respect is to be as specific as your personal interests are. In other words, if you have varied interests that pertain to the program

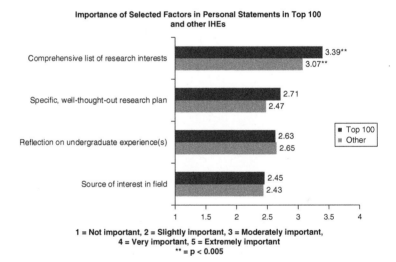

FIGURE 6.2 A comparison of the importance of selected factors in a student's personal statement. Factors were compared separately between the IHEs in the top 100 (dark gray) and IHEs not in the top 100 represented as "Other" (light gray). For both groups, a "Comprehensive list of research interests" was weighted as the most important factor in a personal statement. Asterisks represent significant differences between factors.

you are applying to or the advisor you are applying to work with, mention each of them, highlighting this as an asset in that you are happy to work on varied projects. Alternatively, if you have a specific idea for a project that is relevant, describe it in some detail, showing that you know what you want to do *and* how to do it. Essentially, graduate programs want to know that you have invested some thought into your future and thus have some idea of why you want to go to graduate school and what you expect to get out of it. It is important to realize that each personal statement should be tailored to the specific program you are applying for and/or the researcher you are applying to work with. You should *not* have a blanket personal statement to use for all the different programs you are applying to, even if they are similar.

The personal statement offers an ideal opportunity to address any weaknesses in your application. While not necessarily wanting to draw special attention to your shortcomings, it's important to address any glaring issues and to be upfront about them. For example, if you decided late in your academic career to be a science major, or later in your adult life on a career in science, you can use your statement to write about what inspired your interest in the topic, what you have accomplished since making the decision to pursue science, and what your plans are for your future scientific career. You can also, and should, use this opportunity to discuss skills and experiences you *do* have, which may be more important than those you lack. This is your opportunity to play up your strengths. Your CV is a snapshot of your professional life, but your personal statement is your story, and should be just that, personal. What sets you apart from the other applicants? Spend some time before sitting down to write your statement to answer this question, and let it serve as the thesis for why you are a sound scientific investment.

Some graduate applications will require additional writing samples or at least have the option to upload more writing samples if you so choose. Pay attention to the specific application requirements for the program(s) to which you are applying because writing samples in addition to your personal statement may be required. This is also a great opportunity to submit any other writing samples you may have, particularly if you have any peer-reviewed scientific publications. Remember, anything that conveys your aptitude as a scientist is worth showcasing in your graduate application.

6.6 Nontraditional Student Considerations

While undergraduates may have a hard time generating enough relevant work experience to include in the employment history portion of their application, nontraditional students may find this is their time to shine. Although you may have been out of the academic life for a while, you have other types of work and life experiences that may put your application above those coming directly from a bachelor's degree. From our survey, on average, more than 30% of graduate students in the USA are students who do not enter the program directly after completing their undergraduate degree. This shows that you are not alone, and that graduate programs do not bias against this. Your time away from education may also have provided you with a pool of people from which to request letters of recommendation. If you have an extensive number of people to choose from, it is recommended that you tailor your application to the specific programs to which you are applying by choosing a variety of writers for the different applications. The one big concern is to have your undergraduate, and master's (if appropriate), transcripts on hand while filling out your application to ensure you have all of the relevant information, including your GPA, which you may have forgotten.

The application process for nontraditional students will be similar to those who apply for graduate school directly out of undergraduate education. The major differences will reside in your awareness of school deadlines and calendars (i.e. your life probably doesn't run on semesters), and the amount of time you have available to complete the application. Given the amount of time between when you finished undergraduate education and when you decide to apply to graduate school, you are likely to have other obligations such as a family, or a demanding full-time job. As such, you will need to be particularly aware of time management when applying.

6.7 International Student Considerations

As with most parts of the graduate application process, language will be the largest hurdle to overcome for international students who speak English as a second language. For all parts of the graduate application we advise finding someone who speaks and understands English fluently to ensure you understand and follow all of the application instructions exactly. If this person is in the sciences, all the better! At the very least ensure your personal statement and any other writing samples are reviewed for not only their content, but also their grammar, preferably by someone who speaks English as their first language, if at all possible. It is also important to encourage your letter writers to do the same, which can be a sensitive subject to bring up. You might want to emphasize to your letter writers that you are applying to schools in the USA and explain that you will have an English-speaking person review your application to encourage them to do the same (maybe even offering your English-speaking person as a reviewer). While the language barrier can be an issue throughout the application process, know that admissions offices are aware of the issue, and if anything, being an international student may increase your chances of acceptance as schools hope to diversify their student body. Of the graduate programs we surveyed, an average of 33% of their students were international, and the vast majority of graduate programs in the USA identify attracting a diverse applicant pool as a pressing issue.[2]

[2] Bell, N. E. (2012). *Findings from the 2012 CGS International Graduate Admissions Survey, Phase I: Applications.* Washington, DC: Council of Graduate Schools.

Conclusion

Now that you have prepared for graduate school and chosen the programs to which you want to apply, it's time to start applying. While the application process can be tedious, it should be undertaken with care. Most of the graduate application will involve filling out the same information repeatedly, such as your basic information and your education and employment history, so we strongly advise having that information on hand to refer to as needed. The letters of recommendation are the most important part of your application, and unfortunately the part most out of your control, but we recommend choosing your letter writers carefully and meeting with them ahead of time to help ensure the strongest recommendations possible. Your personal statement is your chance to discuss your own ideas and goals as a scientist and to really demonstrate who you are as a potential researcher. Take great care in crafting this document because it provides admissions offices with a sense of who you are and remember, this can also be used as a method to address any glaring weaknesses in your application. It is crucial that you pay special attention to fees and deadlines in order to give yourself enough time to turn out the highest quality application(s) possible. Finally, remember that while applying to graduate school may be a bit stressful, try and have fun. This is the beginning of the next stage of your career, and instead of thinking about how not to fail, view it as an opportunity to show how awesome you are!

7

Visiting and Interviews

Confidence has a lot to do with interviewing – that, and timing.
> – Sir Michael Parkinson, CBE, broadcaster, journalist and author.

7.1 Introduction

When you reach the phase where you are visiting institutions, this can be an exciting but stressful period. As an applicant, you will travel to various locations, meet new people, and tour prospective graduate institutions. A visit to a graduate school is generally an indication that the potential major advisor or program you have been communicating with is seriously considering you as a student. The realization that acceptance is close but not yet secured can also be a source of worry. You have already put in a considerable amount of work and do not want to make the wrong impression during the in-person interview.

As Sir Michael Parkinson correctly alludes, success in an interview has a lot to do with the confidence of the interviewee, and you can begin to build confidence for your interview by not stressing out about it. We personally feel that the visit to a graduate school should be one that is enjoyed. Yes, students are critically evaluated during their visit, but it is also an opportunity for you to assess the location and the individuals you would interact with for a number of your future years. Graduate institutions try equally as hard to impress the students they bring in for visits, as the students try to impress them. As a student, it is important to remember that graduate students and graduate schools exist in a mutually beneficial relationship. During a visit you should be sure to meet with the potential advisor and see the facilities, but also meet other graduate students. It is important to know how other students feel about the institution, location, and their advisor; this is where you have the opportunity to get an honest opinion of what it is like to work with a potential advisor and to live in the surrounding community.

7.2 Types of Visits

In general there are two types of visits, an unofficial visit and an official visit. Unofficial visits are more appropriate prior to applying, because they provide an opportunity to decide whether or not you want to apply to a given program. For example, if you have a friend or colleague who works at or is attending a graduate school you are interested in applying to, you could use that connection to unofficially visit before applying; this is a great opportunity to start networking. You can arrange to meet prospective advisors, chat with students, and explore the area to help you better assess if you are interested in applying. The in-person interactions during this unofficial visit can also be an opportunity to enhance your case for acceptance later during the application process, as you present yourself as a scientist and potential student. An official visit mirrors many of the aspects of an unofficial visit except official visits are typically paid for by an entity at the institution, and programs use these visits as a dual opportunity to critically gauge prospective students and also to "sell" their graduate program. During official visits *you* should also be critically assessing the graduate program, potential advisors, the environment, etc. to determine your "best fit" graduate program.

If your prospective graduate institution is footing the bill for your visit, they will work with you to determine a mutually beneficial time for the visit; one where the most people who would have an impact on your graduate career are at the institution for you to meet. Graduate programs encourage, and often financially cover, official visits because these in-person interactions help the program determine your potential as a graduate student; any prospective advisors will use student visits as an opportunity to determine your fit in their laboratory or program, and we encourage you to do the same. If you are not offered an official visit you should inquire about one, and if no funding is available we strongly suggest visiting at your own cost if at all possible. On the whole, we would strongly recommend visiting schools before they make a decision to accept you because it is a great opportunity to strengthen your application through in-person interaction, but more importantly gives you a first-hand account of the graduate program as a whole. The advice outlined in the following sections can be applied to both official and unofficial visits.

7.3 Preparing for a Visit

You will want to be as prepared as possible prior to visiting, particularly if you have not yet been accepted into the program. A great way to prepare is by familiarizing yourself with the research of any potential PIs whose interests align with your own. You can familiarize yourself with the work of specific faculty by reading over their individual web pages, which usually includes their background, a statement of research interests, a description of their lab group and currently funded projects, as well as a list of publications. Some PIs list their CVs on their web pages as well. Reading the most recent publications will give you a sense of what the PI is currently working on and will help prepare you for in-person meetings with potential advisors where you will discuss their research. Browsing through some of their older scientific publications will also provide you with a sense of their general research background and make for useful small talk. You do not need to read all of these papers, but going over their titles and abstracts will give you a sense of the research history and direction of the PI. It is also important to review currently funded projects, which you should look closely at when choosing where to apply.

While knowing what type of work the potential advisor has done in the past is important, thinking about how you will fit into current projects and the research direction of the lab is more relevant. You should start developing ideas on how you can contribute to the research the lab is currently doing, and how you might be able to expand aspects of that research into your own thesis project. Familiarity and knowledge of the PI's research cannot be overstated in its importance when preparing for a visit to the school(s) of your choosing. This is true even in lab rotation programs or similar situations where you do not initially apply to work with a specific advisor; it is still advisable to familiarize yourself with the various research interests and projects of several of the PIs in the program with whom you may be interested in working in the future.

You will also want to research the area in which the graduate school is located. Remember, if you end up attending this school, you will live in and spend a significant amount of time in the city or town in which it is located. You should do a bit of research on housing availability, particularly if graduate housing is not provided, as is often the case. Try to determine the average cost of rent as it relates to locations in and around the graduate institution. Will you be able to ride your bike or walk to campus? Or will you need a car and a parking permit – an added expense? Taking the cost of living into consideration is important on your visits, as it can be a crucial component when ultimately deciding between several different schools (discussed in more detail in Section 5.3 *Stipend Positions vs. Non-Stipend Positions* in Chapter 5: *Funding*).

If you have a significant other who will be relocating with you, employment opportunities for them will be a necessary consideration as well, and can be researched beforehand and then explored during the visit. Religious and dietary needs should also be considered when deciding where you will be living. Research places of worship or specialized restaurants and grocery stores ahead of time and plan to visit them during your stay if these things are vital to you. Graduate institutions can be located in populated areas, but it is also possible the location is more remote and has limited options. The geographical dynamics of the graduate program (i.e. is it based in a city or rural area?) may be an important consideration for you, and anyone relocating with you, and should be explored before and then during your graduate school visit.

7.4 What to Wear and Bring

At most graduate institutions the style of dress worn by students, faculty, and staff varies widely, from business attire down to the very casual. It is best to err on the professional side, as opposed to arriving underdressed, when visiting prospective schools for interviews. While dressing professionally is advised, having a few different clothing options on-hand is also a good idea, depending on the length of your visit. If you are interested in a position that requires fieldwork, bring a field-appropriate outfit, just in case an opportunity arises to join your prospective lab mates on a field excursion or in lab work. You may also be walking around campus extensively, so keep comfort in mind, especially when it comes to shoes. Whether in the field or the lab, close-toed shoes are advised, and may be required, so be sure to take this into consideration and dress appropriately for your visit.

You will probably meet with several PIs, current students, other members of the lab, and even administrators (see Sections 7.5 to 7.8 below). When meeting with various people during your visit, you should be prepared to discuss your educational background, as well as any research experiences you have had. Having hard copies of your CV to be able to provide upon request is a good idea, as is any other literature (e.g. publications) showing your aptitude or demonstrating your experience thus far as a scientist. Remember, graduate programs are viewing potential students from a risk potential perspective, and your goal during the visit is to show them that you are a good investment of time and money. The best way to achieve this is to use the personal interactions during the visit to display your potential as a future successful scientist who will contribute to the reputation of the graduate institution. So remember, boast about your experiences and accomplishments!

7.5 Meeting PIs

As stated above and in previous chapters, you will want to be as familiar as possible with any potential future advisors' research interests, ongoing research projects, and past publications; this is true whether you'll be assigned an advisor before or after enrollment. Increasing your knowledge of their research will impress potential PIs in terms of your preparation for the visit, and will allow you to confidently discuss research ideas for your thesis and your potential as a member of their research team. It is useful to remember that although you are the person who is technically being interviewed, the interview is really a mutualistic interaction. Each side is trying to determine if the other will be a good fit. So we strongly encourage you to ask questions of any potential advisors about their expectations of you as a student, their working style, their availability of funding, etc. From these interactions you can try to gauge their personality and whether or not you think you could successfully work in this person's lab. This is a person you will spend a significant amount of time with over the next two to eight years, so ensuring compatibility between the two of you is important. Having the mentality that you are interviewing just as much as you are being interviewed can help relieve some of the pressure and nervousness, and will help you come up with some interesting questions of your own. Asking questions is also a great way to demonstrate your potential and show that you are a confident future scientist. We also suggest speaking as if your acceptance is a foregone conclusion, even if these interactions take place before your formal acceptance. For example, you could ask, "If I choose to come here…" as opposed to "If I am accepted…"; this is a subtle way to show confidence and emphasize that you are looking for a good match for your graduate education, as opposed to being desperate for any position.

If you are a prospective master's student you should discuss ideas for a thesis with the potential advisor. Often master's students are given a project to work on, while other PIs expect to help the master's students develop a project idea after they arrive. Each of these approaches has differing consequences regarding the amount of time you may spend on your thesis and the availability of funding. If your project is pre-assigned and part of a larger research project in the lab group, funding may not be an issue and you will have the opportunity to finish your degree more quickly. However, if you are expected to design your project after enrollment you may be expected to apply for funding once you arrive, and this could end up resulting in more years spent on your degree. Usually doctoral theses are designed much more independently than at the master's level and are developed primarily by the student, with some input from the PI, but this can vary widely between programs and PIs.

7.6 Meeting the Lab

It is important to meet as many people as possible when visiting prospective graduate schools to get a well-rounded perspective of the graduate experience at that location. We cannot emphasize enough that whether you are a master's or doctoral student you will be spending several years of your life at this place, an experience that will differ from being an undergraduate as you become engrossed in your research project. If you have a potential major advisor that you have applied to work with, you should meet with as many people in that person's lab as possible, both in a group setting and individually. These will be the people with whom you will be working closely. There may be a lab manager or lab technician who you work more closely with than your advisor on a day-to-day basis, in addition to the other graduate students in the laboratory. You need to know that you are compatible with these people as well as the PI. Not only will you want to meet and get to know these people personally and assess how they function as a team, but they will also be able to give you individual perspectives on what it's like to work under that particular PI. What are the expectations of the students on this research team? Does he/she require you to work long hours and weekends? How independently are you expected to work? (i.e. is the PI away from the lab frequently?) Who will you be working with daily? How is authorship of research publications determined? Having some time away from the PI to discuss these topics with the other members of the lab can be beneficial to gain useful insight into the inner workings of the research group. If you meet with other people at the institution outside of the lab group, ask them about the reputation of the particular PI and his or her lab group too. The more information the better!

7.7 Meeting Other Students

While you should meet your advisor's other graduate students, it is useful to meet students in the program from outside of the lab(s) in which you are interested in working. Current students will be able to give you an idea of course requirements and their associated time constraints. You may find that PIs are out of touch with the coursework of their students because they are primarily focused on the research aspects of the graduate education, so talking to other students is extremely beneficial. While graduate education in the natural sciences is primarily focused on the thesis project, most graduate programs have core course requirements, courses that all the students in the program are required to take and are generally taken in the first year or two. There are also usually additional discipline-specific courses as well, that may be taken concurrently or later in your graduate career. The first year may be fairly course-heavy, whereas your remaining time in graduate school will be spent on your thesis project, regardless of whether you are a master's or doctoral student.

Meeting and talking with other students can also provide you with a barometer of how your application compares to students who have been accepted and chosen to enroll. You can ask questions about their experiences of applying to the institution in terms of their academic achievements, prior research experience, and their interactions with PIs and administrators. You can then apply this invaluable information as you continue on your visit and to your application if it has not already been completed and submitted.

In addition to providing you with specific information on course requirements, other students at the graduate program will be able to give you an idea of the entire graduate experience at your prospective school; a useful perspective as you might be a student there in just a few short months! You should meet with as many students as possible, both in prospective advisors' and others' labs. The students in a graduate program contribute significantly to its personality and environment and will give you the best idea of your potential fit into the social side of the institution. Most graduate programs include a graduate student association (GSA), which you may want to become involved in and which could be a valuable source of information during your initial visit. Your professional and personal life for the next few years will revolve around your graduate experience; your fellow students will be your friends, colleagues, and potentially your future spouse. Ensuring you fit into that community is an important consideration.

7.8 Meeting the Administration

Your graduate visit will usually include at least one meeting with an administrator; a person who is not a potential PI but serves on the admissions board (e.g. another senior PI at the institution, Dean of Student Affairs, Vice Dean, etc.). This may be an assessment to determine not only acceptance (if you haven't already been accepted), but also the potential for internal funding via in-house fellowships; the awarding of in-house fellowships can be based solely on GPA and GRE. For master's students, more than 60% of the graduate institutions we surveyed provide full funding, meaning tuition plus a stipend, while more than 95% of programs fully fund their doctoral students. In the vast majority of cases, the department, institution, or program pays for at least the student's first year of funding. As a result, the administration, as well as your potential advisor, is interested in your potential for scientific scholarship. Recall that you are an investment for the graduate program, and as administrators they want to take the lowest risk possible in student selection; they do this by gauging your potential to be successful in their graduate program. This may be the most nerve-wracking part of the interview process, but being prepared to discuss the experiences and education that have provided you with the skills to succeed as a scientist will help you ensure the administrators of the program recognize you as a sound investment.

Be prepared to address any weaknesses you may have in your application, as the administrators will want to get a sense of whether that negative aspect of your application is an important consideration, or has a reasonable explanation. So have well-thought-out justifications, but not excuses, for any low grades in important math or science courses, a lack of research experience, low GRE/GPA, etc. This is an invaluable opportunity to address such weaknesses in your application directly with people who will be making decisions about your admission, and to counter-balance those weaknesses by focusing on your strengths. If this meeting comes after other meetings in which you have already discussed some potential research projects with one or more PIs, you will have those talking points to relate to the administrator as well.

7.9 What Questions to Ask

As stated above, we advise that you think of yourself not only as an interviewee, but also as the interviewer, assessing potential advisors and the program for compatibility with your skill set and long-term scientific and career goals. Ask lots of questions! Asking questions shows that you have done your research, you're prepared, and you're inquisitive, which are all extremely desirable characteristics in a scientist. Ask PIs about their research interests

FIGURE 7.1 Questions to ask as a prospective graduate student. Note that this figure is being sarcastic. Reproduced with permission.

and projects; most scientists love to talk about their work and will speak extensively, but be an active listener by asking insightful follow-up questions. It can even be useful to ask questions you know the answer to as an opportunity to demonstrate that you are actively thinking about their research and to demonstrate your inquisitiveness. If you are nervous, this is also a good strategy to help ease into the conversation. As they are talking, think of ways that your background experiences and skill set could contribute to current or future aspects of their research, specifically how you might expand an aspect of a current project into an independent project on which to base your thesis. The more background research and scientific reading you've done, the better prepared you will be to ask valuable questions that show your potential for scientific scholarship and success.

You will also want to know more about the program itself, about the expectations placed on students, as well as the expectations of students' career goals. When asked about her graduate application experience, Laura said that the most awkward part was "Trying to get students and PIs to be honest/direct with you about funding, how much they work, what to expect, etc." How many course credits are required for the degree you are pursuing? How many thesis or research credits? What duties, in addition to your own project and coursework, are required of you? How many years does the average student take to complete the degree or what is the range? How many years does it take your potential PI's students to graduate? How long does funding last? Will you be expected to serve as a teaching or research assistant as part of your funding commitment? Are you expected to secure outside funding? How and when will you be assigned an advisor? What would be the expectations of you in your advisor's lab (in terms of hours per week)? What about any required travel, either to field locations or scientific conferences? Is travel to conferences funded by the department or advisor? What are most alumni doing now – are they in academia, private-sector jobs, or working for non-government organizations (NGOs)?

The scientific questions you ask during your visit will be important in terms of your success as an applicant, but it's also valuable to ask non-science questions to assess if you like the graduate program. You will want a holistic understanding of life as a graduate student at this program. So you should ask where do most students live (i.e. on or off campus, how far away from the school)? Is health insurance offered, and how comprehensive is the coverage? What is the cost? Would the health insurance cover your spouse or family if you have one? What is the social life (or lack thereof) on or around campus? Do students spend a lot of time together outside of work and classes? Are there opportunities to find roommates among your classmates? Where is the nearest grocery store? The nearest airport? The nearest place of worship? The nearest bar?

7.10 International Student Considerations

As an international student it may be more difficult, and sometimes not possible, to arrange for visits to potential graduate schools, but some of the discussion above is still applicable. The widespread use of video calling, using programs like Skype® and G+®, can make it possible for you to have meetings like the ones discussed above, and you can and should ask similar questions. Because you may not be able to physically visit the campus, it is even more important that you get answers to many of the questions we have discussed in this chapter. If it is not readily offered to you, you should ask potential advisors, and/or administrators that you do talk with via video, for contact information for some current students to discuss what life is like in the program. Communication with these students can then occur via email or over the phone (whichever you are most comfortable with). These interactions would be especially beneficial if some of the students are also international and can relate invaluable information about integrating into this graduate program as a non-USA student. Though it may be a disappointment to not get to have in-person conversations, the virtual method of meeting with people may have an advantage in allowing you to get all of your questions answered. You will be able to prepare ahead of time and have the questions on-hand, or in the case of email communication would have the answers in a saved location to be able to go back to.

As an international student you might also want to ask about the general demographics at a particular program and the larger institution. To give you a sense of what to expect, on average, graduate programs in the USA consist of 33% (SD±19) international students. Adjusting to a new culture can be a challenge; locations with a higher international student footprint will have more experience integrating international students into their program both academically and socially. You may want to address any concerns you have about integrating into this new community from the beginning by asking the PI, administrators, or students what their thoughts are regarding how international students fit into their community.

Conclusion

The visit to potential graduate schools is an important step in the graduate application process; it shows you are being seriously considered as an applicant. It is also an important opportunity for you to assess the schools to see if they are to your liking. This will be your home for the foreseeable future, for at least two years, probably longer, and your experience here will differ markedly from that of an undergraduate. You will become part of this scientific community, both professionally and personally. You will spend long hours in the lab or field, and late nights in the library, but you will also contribute to the social atmosphere of the institution and its contextual make-up. It's important that it's an environment you feel comfortable in and benefit from, to make the next few years not only productive, but also enjoyable.

8

Master's, Doctorate, or Undecided?

A journey of a thousand miles begins with a single step.
— Chinese proverb

8.1 Introduction

Your thesis project will be your *life*, or at least a large part of it for the coming years (see Chapter 10: *The Graduate School Experience*). When working on research projects of similar size to the graduate thesis, traditionally scientists work in collaborative teams, with other lab members and PIs. The graduate student, however, is a lone warrior of sorts, with a certain level of independence and associated ownership of their research project. For doctoral students in particular this also means developing the study and sometimes procuring at least partial funding for the project. This level of independence allows a student to learn all of the intricacies involved in scientific research, but it is a method of scientific investigation that is also time consuming. Coupled with classwork and potential obligations in the lab of the major advisor (that stipend is not as free as you think!), a student's research is like their baby, and can encompass a similar amount of time. As a result of the effort involved, pursuing a terminal degree can appear to be an insurmountable endeavor. The Chinese

THE ORIGIN OF THE THESES

FIGURE 8.1 The origin of the theses. From: www.phdcomics.com, with permission.

proverb cited at the beginning of this chapter rings particularly true for the aspiring graduate student who may be hesitant about the totality of the commitment. Despite the magnitude of the endeavor, you cannot accomplish the goal if you do not start, and you will hopefully find that graduate school is a lot of fun despite all the work!

This chapter will discuss the difference between pursuing a master's and doctoral degree and compare the commitment and independence level required by each. Most programs do not require students to have a master's degree before entering a doctoral program, and others allow students with only a bachelor's degree to start their Ph.D., while others allow the option to start as a master's student and then bypass the master's degree to pursue the doctorate; all three of these approaches will be discussed with accompanying information on the pros and cons of each.

8.2 Differences Between a Master's and a Doctorate

Once you have decided you are going to attend graduate school, and before you begin to apply, you may need to resolve if you are going to pursue a master's or doctorate degree. In medieval times a master's and doctorate were synonymous, but over time the doctoral degree conferred a higher level of education in a discipline. In a general sense, a master's degree indicates that one is proficient in their discipline, whereas a doctorate indicates a higher level of mastery and expertise. Many people desire a doctorate, but few are willing to commit and dedicate the necessary time and energy in the pursuit of one. In order to make this decision it might help if you are able to distinguish between the two in terms of graduate school requirements, and career potential. There are a lot of nuanced dissimilarities between master's and doctoral students, but probably the two biggest differences are time and independence.

Time. This is the obvious difference between the two degrees. Typically a master's will take anywhere from two to three years, and a doctorate can take anywhere from five to seven years, though both these numbers can, and do, vary quite a bit. The doctorate degree takes longer because as a doctoral student you are expected to develop most, if not your entire, dissertation research project, and the depth of this project far exceeds that of a master's degree. Yes, you will be able to bounce ideas off of your major advisor and committee members, but the direction, approach, and originality of the project will be your own. The reasoning behind requiring doctoral students to fully develop their dissertation projects is that they are in training to be independent academic scientists. Developing and implementing a research project is a key component of being an independent scientist. Even though most graduate students do not end up in academia (< 8% of Ph.D. students entering the natural sciences become tenure-track faculty[1]), students develop many of the critical independent thinking skills, philosophies, and approaches of their major advisors, and these characteristics tend to serve them well in other science-based careers. See Appendix, source 30 for a breakdown of where science Ph.D.s end up professionally.

---

[1] Sauermann, H. and Roach, M. (2012). Science PhD career preferences: Levels, changes, and advisor encouragement. *PLoS ONE* 7(5): e36307.

As a master's student your project is at least partially determined for you. Sometimes you may have the option to choose from a suite of project ideas, or there may be one singular project that you are brought in to work on an aspect of. There are master's students who are involved in the development of their thesis or generate their own idea/project, but this is less common. Having a project you can step into and immediately begin working on saves a tremendous amount of time. This format generally allows master's students to avoid the theoretical hypothesis-developing phase of science, and the trial-and-error events that result when a student develops a research project from scratch (though as a master's student you will still experience trial-and-error of your own). The master's project is also of a smaller magnitude than the doctoral dissertation, allowing it to be completed more quickly. This distinction in the depth of projects between the master's and doctorate plays a role in how quickly you finish each degree, but also influences the level of expertise you have at the end of your degree. As a rule of thumb, the more time you spend working on something (in any field), the more proficient you become and the greater expertise you develop. Doctoral students spend a significantly greater amount of time in their degree programs, so it is unsurprising that when they complete their degrees they have a greater mastery of their subject area than master's students.

Independence. When you are in graduate school your major advisor, or the PI you are working under, will provide you with guidance and advice as you mature as a scientist. However, even when factoring in the relative differences in advisor style, the level of oversight/independence you receive will differ depending on whether you are a master's or doctorate student. As we mentioned earlier, a master's student's project is usually either predetermined or developed with the close assistance of the major advisor. Master's projects are often an offshoot of a larger project that a PI has funding for and as a result there may be little wiggle room for master's students to intellectually explore the subject on their own; this lack of independence in project development saves time, but also confines the work of a master's student.

When you are pursuing a doctorate, quite frequently the exact opposite is true. Within the relative expertise of your advisor(s), doctoral students are more free to develop and pursue their own research interests. This is time-consuming and challenging, but is also intellectually stimulating and liberating. As a doctoral student you can follow your research interests, have the independence to develop a research idea and propose hypotheses, and determine the method by which you will conduct the study and who you want to work with. Because you have the freedom and independence to do all of this, it also means you have the responsibility to get it all accomplished. Your dissertation journey usually results in the development of relationships with other scientists through networking, procuring funding to conduct aspects of your project, learning techniques (e.g. statistical, field, or laboratory) to implement in your project, as well as any number of other duties. As you progress through your dissertation your level of independence will grow, and in your latter years you will find yourself turning to your PI less and less for advice, making your own decisions instead, and at times your advisor may even seek you for advice! This is part and parcel of scientific maturation.

The amount of independence Ph.D. students receive can be a negative if the student does not work efficiently with a lack of oversight. If you struggle with little direction and freedom of decisions, this would be something to be conscious of if you are considering entering a Ph.D. program. Starting from scratch to develop and implement a project is time-consuming. Yes, your advisor will be there to oversee your work, but as a doctoral student you will be expected to design and execute your project relatively independently. We should point out that this does not mean you will not have independence as a master's student, but your time is more managed by the major advisor than is the case for a doctoral student. It is an opportunity to gain skills and experiences that will aid you in working more independently in the future.

Following undergraduate education, a master's degree is the next logical step for many individuals interested in a higher level of education in the sciences. Traditionally it was required that students do a "march through the diplomas" going from bachelor's, to a master's, and then ending with a doctorate. Now, it is not uncommon for students to forgo a master's degree and directly pursue a doctorate with only a bachelor's degree. Ninety-seven percent of graduate programs surveyed in the USA stated that they admit students to their doctoral programs without having a master's degree. So skipping the master's degree and pursuing a doctorate directly after undergraduate education is a viable option. Whether or not avoiding a master's is right varies by the individual, and asking yourself the questions addressed in the following sections, can assist you with that decision.

8.3 Career Aspirations

We cannot overstate this; determining your career trajectory plays a large role in which degree you should pursue. There tend to be four general career trajectories for natural scientists: academia, government agencies, private sector, and non-government organizations (NGOs). Within these divisions there are various hierarchies that determine which degree you could possibly pursue. Interestingly, though most graduate students state at the beginning of their degrees that they want to pursue academia, the vast majority (> 92%) do not end up in academic positions (Appendix, source 30). We highlight this as something you may want to keep in mind when contemplating your career goals, and which degree you should pursue.

Academia is the traditional route for natural science students. We say this not because the majority of natural science students end up in academia, but the education and experience you receive in graduate school is generally geared toward training you to become an academic scientist (though most of the skills you learn in graduate school translate to other science-related professions). Within academia the general non-student positions you can hold are as a PI, lab manager, or a technician. We use the term PI in a broad sense here and loosely define PIs as follows: 1) predominantly research professors – common at Research First IHEs, where the position requires cutting-edge research; 2) predominantly teaching professors – where the emphasis is primarily on teaching, and both instruction and research endeavors tend to be at the undergraduate level; 3) a research scientist – generally a non-tenured position, with a sole focus on conducting research.

In the research professor and research scientist role, a large portion of time will be spent ensuring research is conducted; this is the primary focus. This manifests itself through grant writing, managing students and technicians, conducting research, writing scientific papers, etc. Teaching and community engagement (i.e. sitting on committees) is required of both professor roles (the research first and teaching professors), but not usually of the research scientist position. Each of the various PIs can advise students, though this role is generally reserved for the professor positions. In order to be a PI in modern science you must have a Ph.D. If you aspire to any of these PI roles, you will need to get a Ph.D. at some point in your career, though it does not necessitate skipping your master's (discussed below).

Within academia the next two positions are lab manager and technician. As a lab manager you generally have to have a master's degree, though it is not always required. The position is as the name would imply: lab managers run a PI's lab, dealing with the day-to-day activities and ensure the lab is functional in conducting research. Lab managers are heavily involved with the research aspects and also delegate responsibilities and assist with the research of other lab members, including students. The lab manager also tends to be a daily outlet for student questions and assists the PI in the training of graduate students. Finally, a lab technician is the workhorse of the lab, a sorting, counting, "field-warrior" who participates in other hands-on activities in the laboratory on a daily basis. This position often requires a bachelor's degree, though there are a number of lab technicians with master's degrees (varying according to the requirements of the lab and responsibilities of the position). As a technician you can expect a heavy component of field and lab work, and like the lab manager, you get to enjoy the perks of doing research without the responsibility of maintaining funding. PIs are regularly writing grants to support research, personnel, and equipment on top of their other scholarly duties, which is a time-intensive endeavor and can be a stressful obligation. If you enjoy doing research, but would prefer to avoid having to worry about funding and developing research ideas, being a technician or lab manager is a good bet.

We have grouped the government agencies, private sector, and NGOs together because there is a large amount of variation regarding whether or not you need a master's or Ph.D., which is contingent on what position(s) you aspire to. Depending on which sector you want to pursue, a good rule of thumb to help you determine if you might need a master's or a doctorate is: assess where you see yourself in that particular sector (i.e. what position do you strive for?), and then look to see what degree the majority of people in that position have, or what degree is listed as a minimum requirement in job announcements for such positions. Generally speaking, the people in the positions you want are good references for what might be required of you in terms of education and experience. Assessing people in desired positions is a good guideline to help you determine which degree to pursue. For each sector, positions in leadership roles generally require higher degrees, though this is not explicit.

8.4 Starting as a Master's Student and Moving on to a Doctorate

There is a third approach regarding which degree you should pursue, and that is the tactic of entering a program as a master's student with the option to transition into the doctoral program; this switch is predicated on your desire to pursue a Ph.D. and your academic and scientific achievements for the first year or two as a master's student. This is a really useful approach because it allows you to enter into a graduate program without the pressures associated with pursuing a doctorate. If you excel in the program you are essentially rewarded with the option to upgrade to the Ph.D. program, as opposed to completing your master's and then separately applying to a Ph.D. program. This approach, the master's bypass, is a useful strategy for students who are initially unsure of which degree they should pursue or who initially lack long-term funding, but are able to procure it in the first year or two of their master's.

Not every program has a master's bypass option, but the majority of IHEs do. In the USA, approximately 80% of graduate programs surveyed stated that they allow master's students the option to bypass the master's program and pursue a doctorate if they successfully earn enough credits and meet other departmental requirements. Of those that do offer a bypass, sometimes the approach is solely optional (i.e. you can apply to the doctorate program with a bachelor's degree), whereas others require students with only a bachelor's degree to enter as master's students with the option for bypassing to the doctorate program. Typically, if you undertake the master's bypass option to a doctoral program you are not awarded a master's degree. This style of graduate education is attractive to both students and the graduate programs because it minimizes risks on both sides. Instead of having students with only undergraduate degrees enter as Ph.D. students, and worrying about their ability to succeed in the program, students are able to begin at the master's level and earn the right to transition to the doctoral level if they wish to do so and also show academic and scientific promise. For students, it provides time to acclimate to the graduate school environment and helps with the decision process of whether or not they want to take the long route of pursuing a Ph.D., thus protecting both parties.

You may be asking yourself, "How exactly does a master's bypass work?" Good question. Typically you, as an applicant, would be informed that the program you are applying for has the option for master's students to bypass to the Ph.D. program if certain academic requirements are met, and if the major advisor and committee approve of your scientific acumen. Students are informed of this option as early as possible to help with their decision regarding a master's or doctorate, but also to help them structure their project with their major advisor if they think this is a viable option to pursue. If you as a student decided (with the counsel of your potential PI) that you were interested in the option of the master's bypass, you would work with your major advisor to structure your thesis in a manner that would allow it to be easily expanded into a full doctoral dissertation. You should also be aware that if you are seriously considering bypassing, your major advisor might require a bit more independence and responsibility of you, to test your ability to operate as a doctoral student. After a time (generally after your first year but before your third) you can transition to the doctoral program if you test out (take your preliminary or qualifying exams at the doctoral level), are in good academic standing, and receive approval from your advisor and committee members who judge your scientific adeptness.

Students choose the bypass route because it saves times in getting a Ph.D. For example, if you entered into a program that required students who only have a bachelor's degree to enter the master's program, but knew you wanted to get a doctorate, if you completed your master's and then re-applied to the same program and received your doctorate it might take you anywhere from seven to ten years in total to complete your graduate education (both the M.S. and Ph.D.). If you bypassed you could expect to reduce the time spent obtaining your doctorate degree to around five to seven years. For those interested in obtaining a doctorate this seems the logical route, but there are benefits to spending time obtaining a master's as well (outlined in Section 8.5 *Undecided*).

While we view the doctorate as a rewarding journey, we understand that the degree, and the pursuit of the degree, is not for everyone. Pursuit of a Ph.D. requires a fair bit of conviction to overcome the numerous challenges that accompany the many highs you will experience. Given this understanding, the approach of entering as a master's and then bypassing to a Ph.D. program makes a lot of sense. There are a number of reasons that a student's initial graduate school experience may not be positive, aside from the obvious academic and scientific difficulties. The advisor-advisee relationship can be a tumultuous one (see Chapter 4: *Choosing a Graduate Program*), the project may not be of interest, the geographic location of the school may be a poor fit, funding could become an issue, etc. Any number of factors, or combinations of factors, could contribute to a student's lack of desire to pursue or even complete a Ph.D., despite their initial willingness when applying, and is why the proposition of a master's bypass is so appealing. If you entered into a graduate program as a master's student with the intention of bypassing and then decided you were not interested in the Ph.D., you would just complete your master's program, no problem! If you "fail" a Ph.D. program and are awarded a master's, there is sometimes a negative connotation associated with your degree (addressed in more detail in Section 8.5 *Undecided*). By entering as a master's student, you have the opportunity to determine if it is really the educational choice and commitment you want to make and whether the IHE you are at is the place where you want to achieve that goal.

8.5 Undecided

Knowing all of this, there are still people who are undecided about what degree they want to pursue, or the specific topic they want to be devoted to studying. If you are undecided, conventional wisdom suggests pursuing a master's degree. Spending time in a master's program will provide you with exposure and experience to the workings of science, allowing you to essentially "get your feet wet." You will take classes, hone your research skills with more intimate oversight from your PI than in a doctoral program, and begin to integrate into the larger scientific community. As a master's student, you get all of these experiences without the rigor, specificity, and time commitment of a doctorate program. The master's degree allows you to test the waters, and if you obtain a master's degree first you may find that if you enter into a doctorate program you are better prepared than those students who entered straight from their undergraduate education. Receiving a master's before taking the Ph.D. route can also help make you a more competitive candidate for Ph.D. programs. With a stronger background in research, proven success in graduate education, and graduate-level skills, your "risk factor" as a doctoral candidate will be significantly lower if you have already completed a master's program. There is a contrast in the scientific maturity of master's students and those with only an undergraduate background that is attractive to PIs. Master's students have a better understanding of "how science works", already have some formal training, and generally have a better sense of what they want to research. As far as graduate applicants are concerned, those with a master's degree are the least risky option.

Though conventional dogma suggests you pursue a master's degree if you are undecided between the two, the data on financial dynamics seems to suggest a different approach. When surveyed, 66% of graduate programs stated they fully support their master's students. Full support means that a program covers the cost of education (tuition and fees), awards a living stipend (enough to generally support not having to work elsewhere), and provides money for research. However, 95% of graduate programs fully support doctoral students. Now here is where the data gets interesting and has some applicability in your decision-making regarding whether to pursue a master's or a doctorate. When questioned as to whether "students who do not complete the Ph.D. program can be awarded a master's degree if they successfully earn enough credits and meet other departmental requirements," 95% of graduate programs indicated that they could. At face value this would suggest that if you were trying to decide between pursuing a master's or doctorate degree at a specific university and the master's degree is not fully funded (which would have about a 40% probability based on our national survey of graduate programs), you could enter the doctoral program which is likely to be fully funded, and if things did not work out you could still receive a master's degree. This was a surprising finding because we do not think graduate programs actively acknowledge that this is the case, or would suggest this approach, but the data suggests this could be a logical strategy.

Where logic fails is in assessing the reality of this perception. This approach would make a lot of financial sense, but a stigma may be attached to students who are awarded master's degrees after initially pursuing a Ph.D. Some graduate programs solely award Ph.D.s, and having a master's degree from that program is an indication that an individual was unsuccessful in the Ph.D. program. Also this caveated approach can be more of a negative, and could affect your self-confidence going forward. The idea of hedging your bets implies a certain lack of self-assurance, which is vital in completing graduate education at any level. Entering into a master's program and working toward a Ph.D. has a far greater positive connotation, than planning on receiving a master's degree if you are unsuccessful in a Ph.D. program. So choosing to follow the route suggested by the data could be a risky proposition.

Another reason to focus on a master's degree before going for a Ph.D. would be to increase your chances of acceptance into a highly competitive doctoral program. As we touched on before, master's students are generally more scientifically adept than students coming straight from undergraduate education. They have spent more time in their scientific field and know what is expected of them. They also have established relationships with other top PIs and have publications. The IHE where you receive your doctorate tends to be the place people associate with your educational background. If you aspire to attend a top graduate program but do not believe you can do so with your undergraduate achievements, completing your master's can be a great way to build your resume. There is a distinction between what the top 100 IHEs and other IHEs value as important (see Figure 1.2); letters of recommendation and research experience rank very highly. Letters of recommendation were valued as a factor in admissions decisions in general, but when compared by program ranking, those IHEs in the top 100 placed greater emphasis on these letters. The same is true of research experience, where independent and general research experience were more valued by the top 100 IHEs than those outside of the top 100. If you desire to get into a doctorate program at a top 100 IHE, getting a master's degree is an avenue to developing relationships with well-known scientists in your field who can write you a letter of recommendation; completion of your master's thesis is also a strong indication of your aptitude for scientific research. So if you need time to gain more research experience or develop relationships with letter writers, obtaining a master's degree is a great stepping-stone.

Conclusion

Graduate school is a unique experience, and deciding which degree you want to pursue is one of a long list of important considerations. Should you pursue a master's or doctorate? It can be a tough decision because the person you are now, and the career desires you have, may change after your first couple of years in graduate school. Which degree you choose to pursue will have a big impact on the amount of time that you spend in graduate school, as well as the amount of work that will be required of you. Pursuing a Ph.D. requires a serious amount of commitment because the effort required to develop a research project, implement that research plan, and analyze and synthesize the results is no small order. Pursuing a master's is no small order either; two to three years is still a significant chunk of your life.

Whichever degree you decide to pursue, we believe you will find the experience rewarding, and with perspective, most people look back fondly on their time in graduate school.

9

Acceptance and Decision Time

Decisions are the hardest thing to make, especially when it is a choice between where you should be and where you want to be.

– Anonymous

9.1 Introduction

The hard work is over (for now) and the important decision of which institution to attend needs to be made. Choosing a graduate program from the ones that have accepted you is not as easy as it sounds. When asked about a regret in her graduate school experience, one student said, "Not talking to the students in the lab before accepting, and not waiting to hear back from both schools. I should have held my ground longer until I had all the information." This decision commits you to a specific location and to working with specific people, the major advisor in particular, for a number of years of your foreseeable future. Because of the magnitude of the decision, the quote at the beginning of this chapter echoes our sentiment that this is not a decision to be made lightly. However, the information you have learned in this book should provide you with confidence that you have all the tools to make the best decision from your available choices. In this chapter, we will summarize and review a number of important considerations to make when deciding on a graduate program, which were outlined in more detail throughout the previous chapters of this book.

9.2 Factors to Consider in Your Decision

Upon receiving your acceptance letters the first step is to cheer, WOOT! You are wanted! Acceptance letters and offers of scholarships and stipends are generally sent during the spring semester, usually in March or April, with decisions on where to enroll to be made sometime in May, but this does vary. The next step is to decide which of your accepted graduate programs you are seriously considering. Knowing which programs you have been accepted to may cause changes in your perceived "best" IHE. When you initially applied to graduate school you may have sent in a large number of applications or included a few "safe bet" schools where you were confident in your acceptance. You may have also had preconceived notions about programs based on their reputations, potential PIs, funding, research projects, location, etc. As a result, this information was probably used to informally (or for the more organized applicant, formally) rank these schools. Now that you have been accepted and have visited some, if not all, of the programs and exchanged correspondence with each IHE, your initial perceptions about each place may have changed so you should rearrange the hierarchy of the programs you want to attend and attempt to narrow it down to two or three.

Once you have narrowed down the list of schools to those that you are most interested in attending, if you have not already done so you should try and visit those programs. This will help you get a feel for not only the program and its participants, but also the local community that you will be living among and contributing to over the next few years. In-person familiarity with the location and program can be a crucial component of your decision-making process. You want to make the most informed decision possible, and that includes knowing the people and the place. On your visit you will want to be sure to meet with potential major advisors, and members of the lab group, but you should also try to meet with other professors, administrators, and students (see Sections 7.5 to 7.9 in Chapter 7: *Visiting and Interviews*). Remember, when meeting with current students, ask them about their experiences at that respective graduate program, both the positives and negatives. Different students will have varying opinions and experiences; by asking several students their thoughts and feelings about their time at the prospective IHE, you will be able to gain a more holistic sense of the graduate experience at that IHE.

In addition to engaging with the graduate community, if you are able to you should also spend some time in the local community to get a feel for the area in which you will be living. Visit places you would want to live, grocery shop, and enjoy recreational activities, as the availability of these things may be important to you in your years in graduate school and can vary by location.

Once you have been accepted, it will be important to seriously consider your feelings about each of the individual programs, including the potential major advisors, lab groups, and various projects you are considering. Your comfort level at the IHE and your interactions with people during your visit is important. If you are pursuing a doctorate you might spend almost twice as much time in your graduate program as you did at your undergraduate institution, so you want to choose a location you can picture yourself living in, working, and growing as a scientist, and you want to be surrounded by individuals who will foster that professional and personal growth.

You will also want to compare the financial packages that are being offered by the IHEs that accepted you. Funding is a hugely critical component of the graduate process, and should be a major consideration in your decision-making of where to attend. Unlike medical school and law school, attendance at thesis-based graduate programs typically does not add to the student loan debt you may have accrued as an undergraduate. According to our survey, over 60% of IHEs offer stipends plus tuition to master's-level students, and more than 95% to doctoral-level students. If one program is offering full funding, stipend plus tuition, whereas another is only offering tuition help in the form of a scholarship, it may make your decision much easier. You might also take into consideration the difference in the stipends offered. However, remember that stipend differences are relative to the cost of living (COL) in the area surrounding the IHEs under consideration. There are online COL calculators to directly compare stipends and salaries in various cities (see Appendix, source 11). Twenty thousand dollars a year will go much further in Gloucester Point, Virginia than it will in San Diego, California! The absence of a stipend or the guarantee of a stipend for all your graduate school years should not immediately preclude a graduate program, but should be a factor in your comparison of programs. Even if you are offered a stipend and tuition at an institution, how many years of that is guaranteed? Will you need to apply for additional funding later in your graduate career?

The cost of rent is an important component of the COL, and exploring your living options at the schools you've narrowed your list down to can also help you compare the true value of various stipends. You will also want to consider your commute – will you need to own a car? Or can you rely on public transportation? What will be the cost in terms of fuel and vehicle maintenance, or a bus or subway pass? Also remember that time is money; how long will your commute be? If it's a long commute, but includes public transportation, can you use that time to work, research, or answer emails? In addition to local travel, you may want to consider the cost of travel home, wherever that may be. Is it within driving distance? Or will it require the purchase of a plane ticket a few times per year? Another consideration is whether the graduate program covers healthcare costs. Depending on your health, or whether or not you have a family, this could be a major sticking point, but should be factored into the pros and cons of each school you are considering regardless. Unexpected medical expenses are always a possibility, so comparing the cost and level of coverage is worthwhile. What are the premiums and deductibles? What percentage is covered for in network versus out of network physicians? Also, is vision and dental insurance included?

In addition to considering the funding that has been offered to you in terms of tuition and stipend, you will want to consider the available funding for your research project. Are you jumping into a project that has already been funded for a number of years and the grant may be winding down, or will the funding be starting when you arrive? Do you even have funding? A lot of the availability for funding will revolve around if you are adding to or developing a thesis around the initial statement of work for an existing grant. The alternative is designing your own research project, with the expectation that you would need to procure additional funding once you have enrolled. Which of these options is more desirable to you? Does this differ at the institutions you are considering after acceptance? Is there potential to expand a master's thesis into a full doctoral dissertation (i.e. master's bypass)? All of these questions can affect the time you spend earning your degree and should be considered alongside your future scientific goals. Realizing you might have to write one or several grants while in graduate school can be a benefit, because it will provide you with grant writing experience, plus give you the freedom of having monetary control (explained in detail in Chapter 5: *Funding*). However, grant writing is time consuming, so you need to evaluate the pros and cons of these two options and how they fit into other attributes of a graduate program when making your decision.

9.3 Making the Choice

When comparing the various IHEs you have been accepted to, it is important to think about the long-term success of former students. Some IHEs will post lists of what graduates are doing now, which can be very helpful for gauging whether a given school has a record for producing successful students. Although your career goals may change throughout your graduate education, they should be at the forefront of your mind throughout the graduate application process, particularly now that you've reached decision time. Are the schools you have been accepted to mostly preparing students for academia? Or are there a wide variety of possible career paths that graduates have taken? While it may seem a long way off at the moment, your graduate education should prepare you for the type of scientist you want to be and for success in the job of your choosing; the careers of a scientist, even in a given field, can vary widely. If you are not interested in academia you want to make sure you enroll in a graduate program that exposes its students to other career avenues in science, so that you do not feel unguided about how to transition from graduate education to your desired career path. If a convenient list of "Where are they now?" graduate students is not located on the school's website, these are questions worth asking during the interview process or when visiting, whether your visit occurs before or after acceptance. When addressing these questions, you could ask: What percentage of graduates go on to secure postdoctoral positions? How many work for government agencies? How many former students are teaching or otherwise employed at other IHEs? Do advisors have career expectations for their students? If so, how rigid are they? This can be a big one; many advisors want to produce "mini-mes," and expect their progeny to carry on their academic legacy and further their work. Understanding expectations from a potential PI and realizing your own scientific career desires can be important when selecting a graduate program.

Whether you choose a PI before or after your acceptance to graduate school, your advisor will often be one of the most important people for helping you chart your career path. This increases the importance of maintaining an open dialogue about career desires and expectations. Additionally, the way an advisor approaches mentoring a student who is interested in pursuing academia, compared to one interested in a non-academic career, may differ as each career has varying skill and résumé requirements.

You should also consider the size of a potential lab and the advisor's mentoring style. Would you prefer an advisor who is hands-off, extremely involved, even keel, or able to spend a significant amount of time guiding you? These are all important considerations. An advisor managing a large lab with lots of students, technicians, and obligations will not have as much time to personally interact with you. Is this okay for you? You should observe and make note of the current status of students in the lab you would be joining. How many students does the PI currently have and what have previous students gone on to do professionally? Does the prospective advisor maintain relationships with former students either personally or professionally? Are the students happy? If you have the opportunity, it would be worthwhile to contact former students about their experiences at the school, with the advisor, and to inquire as to where their graduate education has taken them.

Another important aspect when deciding between schools is assessing how long it takes students to complete their degree. Most master's programs take two to three years, but are students finishing in the projected time frame? Or are most taking longer? Doctorates vary more widely, anywhere from four to nine years, but you should know where on that spectrum most students in the program (or even more specifically, the lab you are interested in) take to finish their degree. Additionally, most graduate programs have official expectations for how long it should take students to complete a degree, and you should compare the programs you are considering to find out this information.

Conclusion

Celebrate, you have earned it! At this stage you have successfully navigated the application process and are in the somewhat less stressful position of deciding between programs that are now competing for *your* acceptance. Now is the time to really evaluate the best fit in terms of your long-term professional goals and your comfort at an IHE: in the program, in the community, and with any potential major advisors. The fact that you will spend a large portion of your time embedded in this community cannot be overemphasized, but the proverbial ball is now in your court and it's your turn to decide which program best fits *you*. This is the enjoyable part. All the hard work has paid off, and now you get to decide where the next chapter of your life begins. Good luck!

10

The Graduate School Experience

I went to graduate school and there it all happened.
> – Ted Nelson, American author

10.1 Introduction

Nelson's quote appropriately summarizes the scientific and personal maturation that many students undergo during their time in graduate school. In our survey of current and former graduate students, when asked to describe their graduate school experience in one word respondents used words like "time-consuming," "lengthy," "stressful," and "overwhelming," but also "challenging," "exciting," "competitive," and "manageable." Graduate school is more than an education, it is also a location where you as a student will spend three to eight years of your life, growing and maturing as a scientist and as a person. Because of this, it is important for you to consider your personal life when making decisions about where to attend school, to better ensure happiness and success during your graduate school tenure. Things to consider are the cost of living and standard of living (e.g. a $20,000 stipend offered in New York City is worth much less than a $19,000 stipend in Bowling Green, Ohio), nearby markets for food (particularly if there are special dietary restrictions), and your

FIGURE 10.1 From cheeky to geeky: the evolution of your sense of humor in graduate school. From: www.phdcomics.com, with permission.

comfort level in the adopted community. Graduate students with a family (or those who may start one while in graduate school) also need to consider whether there are job opportunities available for your spouse or significant other, as well as family-friendly policies at the school and in the surrounding community.

While the main focus of this book is the graduate application process, this chapter will briefly provide advice about the graduate school experience.

10.2 The Local Community

A significant aspect of your graduate school experience, as it relates to your social well-being, will be the surrounding community in which you live. The social demographics of a community vary by location, and it may be difficult to fully grasp the dynamics of the community during your official visit. As a result, once you are permanently settled at the location of your graduate program, you should go and explore your new home. The members of your graduate program, and the IHE as a whole, are likely to form the foundation of your social life. However, it can also be important to take advantage of social opportunities and outlets outside of your graduate program for a more holistic experience. Determining what kind of community or lifestyle you will enjoy does require a bit of introspection.

Once you have moved, it is then time to determine the best way to interact and engage with your new community. This can be a daunting task, so partnering with other students to attend local social outings (e.g. bars, festivals, community markets) is a good idea. Having a life outside of graduate school is good because when things get stressful in your graduate program, it is nice to have an outlet to "escape" to. Plus, by being involved and connected with the community in which you live, it can provide a sense of comfort that should help you settle into your graduate program. We can't say this enough; being happy in your community is a key component of being happy in your graduate program.

10.3 If You Have a Family

It can be difficult to maintain a family while in graduate school. Pursuing a graduate degree requires a fair bit of self-sacrifice, while a family is largely about compromising your time for the greater good of the family. Balancing the need to be selfishly consumed with your graduate work, along with the responsibilities of your family, is not impossible, but will require a bit of diligence. Know you are in good company; many people successfully complete graduate school while still maintaining a family. The best advice to give in this regard is to have open communication with your significant other and to be very organized with your time, a great skill to hone for any scientist. As you deal with the rigors of graduate education, be open and honest with your partner about what the demands are on your time, and how you are managing so many obligations. Similarly, listen to how your time demands are impacting your significant other. This open communication from both parties should foster a better understanding of what the other is going through, and lead to cooperative approaches to address conflicts. There are inevitably going to be occasions where your time is pulled more in the direction of graduate school: think final exam time. However, because you have time obligations at home as well, to ensure that you have an equitable distribution of your time spent on your home life and graduate education, thoroughly organize your schedule with your partner. These simple approaches should help alleviate the stress that could arise with managing your graduate education and a family.

10.4 Extracurricular Activities

When asked about regrets in graduate school, Dr. Leah Zullig, now an assistant professor at Duke University, stated, "I enrolled in a top-notch and very intense Ph.D. program and completed it in 3.5 years. I graduated with lots of publications and excellent contacts, but I was exhausted. It's important to take time for yourself. Graduate school isn't everything ... it's just one aspect of life." Graduate school cannot be all work, despite what your advisor may assert. You need to have a healthy balance of work and social activities to have a productive graduate school existence. Make sure you prioritize time to maintain your favorite hobbies (or pick up new ones). If you like to run or play soccer, don't stop doing these activities because of the time they will take away from you graduate work; you should make a concerted effort to fit them into your schedule. Your hobbies are a part of who you are, and by continuing them you maintain a part of your identity. Additionally, because these are activities you enjoy, your involvement will undoubtedly contribute to stress reduction in your life. If you have a hobby that is not as ubiquitous as soccer, let's say you play lacrosse instead, do not be discouraged. You might have to get a bit more creative about how you can still enjoy this activity (depending on your location). Maybe the university has a lacrosse team and you can practice with them (or a local grade school)? Or maybe a neighboring city has a lacrosse club. It would require traveling, but could be worth it for something you enjoy. For your hobbies you have to be somewhat vigilant about how you can maintain them in graduate school. You are going to be making a lot of self-sacrifice for your academic degree, and in order to maintain a healthy mental balance try to identify opportunities that allow you to take time away from work and participate in something you enjoy.

Although the preceding advice used sporting examples, this suggestion extends to any and all activities that are important to you. If spiritual worship is key, make sure that you allocate time in your schedule to find a place of worship and participate in that community. Additionally, if other artistic endeavors like joining a dance group or open mic are important, most definitely strive to engage in those activities as much as you can. Your intellectual well-being in graduate school will be greatly enhanced by your social well-being.

While you want to make time to participate in activities that you have a familiarity with, do not be afraid to try new things! Graduate school, like undergraduate education, brings people together from all different walks of life, and you will have the opportunity to join others in their passions. Participating in activities in which you might not have the best skill or experience will still connect you with your peers and makes for a great social foundation with people in the surrounding community or others at your IHE.

10.5 International Student Considerations

As an international student, one of the challenges you may face in graduate school is adapting to American culture, especially if American culture drastically differs from your own. Instead of thinking of it as a challenge, try and perceive it as a new adventure and have fun with it. There may be language barriers, especially when it comes to jokes or jargon. To help bridge these cultural barriers you can watch movies and TV, have random conversations with people, and don't be afraid to ask if you do not understand something. Remember that on average international students make up 33% of graduate students at USA graduate programs, so you are not alone and may find comfort in seeking out other international students for camaraderie.

You should also be aware that within a university "bubble" the ideology is generally quite liberal and open, but outside of this environment (depending on which region in America you are living), people's philosophies and perspectives could drastically differ. For example, you may take for granted that people from your country generally accept the science behind climate change, and this may be reinforced at your USA graduate university. However, for example, if your university is located in the southeastern USA, you may find that many people in the surrounding community of your graduate program do not share this view. This should not be a major issue, but do be aware that seemingly obvious viewpoints you share with your science colleagues and friends and family back home might be somewhat culturally contentious in certain communities in the USA.

You may also experience homesickness, especially during the early part of your time away. If it is feasible, do not hesitate to go home when needed. Going home may be necessary to maintain a sense of equilibrium, but more importantly making friends in your new location will go a long way to alleviating homesickness and help you establish a life in your new home. As you make friends and adapt to your new culture, you don't want to lose your identity; you want to maintain a balance between remaining connected with your own culture and assimilating into the local culture. Sharing your culture or cultural practices with your new friends is a great way to stay connected with your roots while also exposing your new friends to an aspect of who you are and where you come from.

If you have access to other international students, they are a great support, especially during American holidays when a lot of other people at your program may go home. Additionally, some of the more senior international students can provide you with specific advice about how to tackle or deal with issues that may arise, and more importantly these individuals can serve as a sympathetic ear as you adjust to your life in the USA. It may be rough at first, transitioning to graduate school while having to manage a new language and culture. However, lots of international students have successfully navigated this hurdle, and as a result, your own life, and the lives of those around you, will be more enriched by this cultural diversity.

Conclusion

Graduate school is a wonderful experience full of social and intellectual stimulation. You are in a cerebral environment full of creativity and rigor. At the end of this journey you will have established relationships with people that will last the rest of your life. Most people look back on graduate school fondly, and so the best advice we can give is to fully embrace the experience and enjoy the ride while it lasts!

Appendix

#	Title	url
1	ETS Graduate Record Examination (GRE)	www.ets.org/gre
2	*POWERPREP® II, Version 2.2 Software: Preparation for the Computer-delivered GRE® revised General Test*	www.ets.org/gre/revised_general/prepare/powerprep2
3	Register for the GRE	www.ets.org/gre/revised_general/register/?WT.ac=grehome_greregister_b_150213
4	Kaplan GRE Test Prep	www.kaptest.com/gre
5	The Princeton Review GRE Test Prep	www.princetonreview.com/grad/gre-test-prep
6	ETS TOEFL iBT® Test	www.ets.org/toefl
7	Science Direct	www.sciencedirect.com
8	Google Scholar	https://scholar.google.com
9	National Science Foundation Award Search	www.nsf.gov/awardsearch/
10	National Institute of Health Award Search	http://projectreporter.nih.gov/reporter.cfm
11	Nerdwallet COL Calculator	www.nerdwallet.com/cost-of-living-calculator/?trk=nw_gn_3.0
12	National Science Foundation Graduate Research Fellowship	www.nsf.gov/funding/pgm_summ.jsp?pims_id=6201
13	National Institute of Health Graduate Research Fellowship	www.training.nih.gov/programs/gpp
14	Fogarty International Center Life Science GRFs	www.fic.nih.gov/FUNDING/NONNIH/Pages/predoctoral-graduate.aspx

#	Title	url
15	National Oceanic and Atmospheric Administration GRF	www.epp.noaa.gov/ssp_grad_sciences_page.html
16	Environmental Protection Agency GRF	www.epa.gov/ncer/fellowships/
17	NSF Broader Impacts	www.nsfgrfp.org/#impacts
18	Examples of NSF project proposals	https://docs.google.com/spreadsheets/d/1xoezGhbtcpg3BvNdag2F5dTQM-XI2EELUgAfG1eUg0s/edit#gid=0_
19	National Physical Science Consortium GRF	www.npsc.org
20	Ford Foundation GRF	http://sites.nationalacademies.org/PGA/FordFellowships/PGA_047959
21	University of California, Santa Cruz Compilation of Minority GRFs	http://graddiv.ucsc.edu/financial-aid/minority-fellowships.html
22	UniGo Scholarship Directory	www.unigo.com/scholarships#fromscholarshipexperts
23	Fulbright Fellowship	http://foreign.fulbrightonline.org
24	Leo. S. Rowe Pan American Fund	www.oas.org/en/rowefund/FinancialGuideForHigherEducation.pdf
25	Aga Khan Foundation	www.akdn.org/akf_scholarships.asp
26	American Association of University Women	www.aauw.org/what-we-do/educational-funding-and-awards/international-fellowships/
27	Education USA	https://educationusa.state.gov
28	International Student Exchange & Study Abroad Resource Center	www.internationalstudent.com
29	Educational Testing Service (ETS)	www.ets.org/
30	Science Career Paths by the Numbers	http://ascb.org/where-will-a-biology-phd-take-you/

Index